Estranged

Finding Hope When
Your Family Falls Apart

JULIE PLAGENS

Copyright ©2019 by Julie Plagens. All rights reserved. All Scripture quotations, unless otherwise indicated, are taken from the Holy Bible, New International Version®, NIV®. Copyright ©1973, 1978, 1984, 2011 by Biblica, Inc.™ Used by permission of Zondervan. All rights reserved worldwide. www.zondervan.com The "NIV" and "New International Version" are trademarks registered in the United States Patent and Trademark Office by Biblica, Inc.™ Scripture quotations marked (NLT) are taken from the Holy Bible, New Living Translation, copyright ©1996, 2004, 2015 by Tyndale House Foundation. Used by permission of Tyndale House Publishers, Inc., Carol Stream, Illinois 60188. All rights reserved.

Book design by Five J's Design, FiveJsDesign.com

This book is dedicated to my husband, Andy. Thank you for being there in the hard times and loving me through it.

Special thanks to Dr. Deborah Newman for helping me when I didn't know what to say.

Estranged

TABLE OF CONTENTS

Join the Mom Remade Community 9
Introduction. 11

CHAPTER 1	Sick of It All.........................	**15**
CHAPTER 2	Leaving a Christian Family............	**25**
CHAPTER 3	Estranged from Family...............	**35**
CHAPTER 4	Retaliation Never Works.............	**49**
CHAPTER 5	The Consequences of Estrangement	**57**
CHAPTER 6	The Real Problem with Families	**67**
CHAPTER 7	I Choose to Forgive	**83**
CHAPTER 8	Reconciliation: Eight Miracles	**95**
CHAPTER 9	Coming Home to Family.............	**109**
CHAPTER 10	When God is Silent	**119**
CHAPTER 11	How to Heal from the Pain............	**129**

Afterword: An Interview with Julie's Mother............ *141*
About Julie Plagens. *153*

JOIN THE
Mom Remade Community

About a year ago, I dropped my last child off at college. It was a bittersweet moment. I was glad to release her into adulthood, but I was also sad because I was technically out of a job. I no longer had anyone at home who needed a full-time mom. On the long drive home, I asked God what He wanted me to do now that I was an empty-nester. Unlike some of my prayers that had taken years to be answered, this one God answered immediately.

His Spirit quietly spoke to me while we were driving. He said to tell other moms about Him. It wasn't a big, loud voice. It was a sudden "knowing." Specifically, He said to tell them how to raise godly children. He reminded me that I struggled with parenting not so long ago as a young mom and could have used some encouragement when I was down in the trenches. After that revelation in the car, I knew I needed to go back and tell others what I had learned as a parent and about my own struggles with my family of origin. I figured if God was in it, someone would listen. Surely there was somebody who had struggled through some of the same issues I had.

It's been just over a year now. In this time, I have written two books. I also manage my website and maintain all the social media accounts connected to my blog. My mission has been to provide a place online where other moms can find parenting and family advice with biblical wisdom. I also hope to offer encouragement and validation related to struggles with families of origin. All I can say is that God did it. Not me. I had no technical skills when I started, and it had been 25 years since I had written anything worth reading.

If you would like to check out the other things I have written, here is the link to my book *Creating Family Memories: How to Make Family Time with a Crazy Schedule*. You can buy it on Amazon or through other eBook sources. You can check out my blog at *MomRemade.com*.

I have a Facebook group for parents of pre-school kids and older called Christian Parenting and Family at *facebook.com/groups/628239597606364/*.

Introduction

You may wonder why I would write a book about such a messy subject. No one in her right mind would want to bring up past hurts and talk about them publicly. It could cause another family split. I agree. It is risky, but my family has been very supportive along the way. They have sent me information to include in my book and have proofed it several times to help guide me in the right spirit.

In fact, the afterword is written by my mother. I wanted others to hear her perspective. It is important that both sides of this topic are addressed. I am grateful my mom has taken the time to give her thoughts on our estrangement.

I decided to write this book because I found very little written on the subject of family estrangement, specifically from a Christian perspective. When I left my family, I found no books in the bookstore close to my situation and very little online that talked about Christian families being estranged. Yet, here I was, a Christian, reeling from the pain, and no one could answer my questions. The books I did find about estrangement were from psychologists who retold stories about their patients, angry women who were never going back, and others with stories but no biblical viewpoint. None of their stories were like mine.

I was looking for a person who had been estranged from family and who had worked through the situation with complete forgiveness. I needed to hear a Christian talk about this subject. I am not only a Christian, but I also come from a family in ministry. I am a preacher's kid. Perhaps God could use my story to pull the curtain back and reveal the truth. The truth is we are all sons of Adam and subject to the Fall. There are no perfect families, mine included.

I do not want to portray my family in a bad light. My intention is for you to see God glorified in a messy situation. He alone is the Author and Hero of this story. He is to be praised for all the healing that has happened between my family and me. God is the only one who can soften hardened hearts and bring life back into dead relationships. He can do the same for you that He has done for us. Our Heavenly Father is no respecter of persons.

This book lists actionable steps to help you move toward healing and restoration, whether you are the parent or the child. These steps will help you work toward forgiveness and change the way you feel about your family members even if there is never complete restoration. The steps are not easy, but they work. No matter where you are in the process, whether it is a strain in the family or a complete family break, you can move to a better place than where you are right now.

I would like to add that although you may be going through a difficult family situation and are physically and emotionally sick, you should recognize that good medical advice should be sought. This book is not intended and should not be construed as a substitute for medical care.

I pray my words will give you hope for your own situation and help you know you are not alone. There are a lot of other people just like you who have family issues. They just don't talk about it. I want my story to help you see there is a way out of your pain. God can use your brokenness for His glory if you will let Him.

CHAPTER 1

Sick of It All

I woke up from anesthesia and heard the words, "You have Crohn's disease." The nurse went on: "You are probably going to lose your colon and will have a bag for an intestine for the rest of your life. The doctor is going to have to take out the lower portion of your colon. It is diseased and looks like hamburger meat."

That was not exactly what I was hoping for when I woke up, but I wasn't surprised. Actually, I was grateful the doctor didn't find cancer. I was sure that was what was wrong with me. But removing my colon didn't sound much better. I didn't want to have a bag attached to my side for the rest of my life. The combination of the smell, the noises, and the utter shame was more than I could handle. I would never want to go in public again. And what about my marriage? That was even more frightening. I knew my husband would love me, but I would be embarrassed to be intimate with that kind of alteration to my body.

I had been so sick for the last three months and was positive I would not live another year. I had lost 30 pounds in that short time. Nothing would stay in my stomach. Everything I ate came right back out. I couldn't even drink water without ill effects. I was slowly wasting away.

As I was lying in bed that day in the hospital, I knew what was wrong with me. The denial left, and my eyes were opened. I could no longer run from the real problem. I was angry. I wasn't just a little angry; I was filled with bitterness and hatred. It was a deep, dark feeling I could no longer control. The bitterness had been simmering in my heart for years. I could no longer keep up the facade.

From the outside, it looked like I was okay. Not physically okay, but at least emotionally okay. I had done an excellent job of hiding my feelings from everyone. No one knew what was going on in my heart. The truth was I was tired of living one way and feeling another. Our family had problems, and no one was talking about them. The problems had been there for so long that it was normal. But our normal was not healthy. Over the years, I had tried to push back against the unrealistic expectations I felt had been put on me, but I was met with a lot of resistance. I felt like no matter what I did, it was not good enough.

Right there in the hospital bed I decided to cut off my relationship with my parents. I didn't know how I would do it at the time. That didn't matter to me. I just knew I had to leave my family to get well. At the time, I didn't realize I had a natural tendency to run and hide when I couldn't resolve my problems. As a child, I loved making secret hideouts outside or secret forts in my closet. It was my way of coping with my family. By the time I became an adult, running and hiding was second nature to me. It just felt like the normal thing to do when there was no way out. In the hospital, I came to the conclusion I was mentally and physically exhausted from trying to jump through all the hoops. I was done.

After I made this decision, I decided I didn't care what people thought. This was huge for me, because I always cared what everyone thought. I am a people-pleaser to the core. I was so sick that I didn't care what it took for me to get well. I didn't care if my church banned me, or my friends left me. I didn't care if I had to run to Mexico. I was going to leave my family and get free. I wanted to be free from the entangled relationship we had and the pain it was causing me physically, mentally, and emotionally. I am not blaming my parents for my illness. That was on me. My biggest problem was the way I coped with emotional pain. It was not healthy. The only way I knew to break the pattern was to walk away. I needed to find out who I was as a person and a Christian outside of my family of origin. I wanted to find me outside of them.

My Family

My family was well known in the Dallas area when I was growing up. The Ventura name was synonymous with live entertainment and Italian food. My parents owned the Italian Village restaurant, Club Village (the first supper club in Dallas), and Gringos (the first disco/nightclub in Texas). This made my parents wealthy in their early twenties. It was a lot for them to handle at such a young age. They would be the first to say that the fame was hard on the whole family. Some family members were jealous, and other family members were angry. I'm sure many were wondering how a 23-year-old kid hit it so big. Things like this usually didn't happen. There was no way to prepare for that kind of money and responsibility. My parents were pulled in so many directions trying to manage a business that exploded overnight.

For many years, the Italian Village was one of the best places in Dallas to have a good time and eat an amazing Italian meal. There was very little competition in the area. They dominated the nightclub industry in Dallas. Even stars from Hollywood and Las Vegas would eat at their restaurant when they were in town. Their bar was the only place in Dallas to watch the Dallas Cowboy game on television during a blackout. This concept was a forerunner to the sport's bars of today. When the Dallas Cowboys weren't playing, the players would often come in and hang out in the bar area or eat at the restaurant. The Italian Village was the place to be in the 1960s and 1970s.

After about ten years of living in the fast lane, my dad found he was empty. He had accomplished about everything he could in his field. There were no challenges left. He started asking God if there was more. He prayed and asked God to show him if He was real. My father was a Catholic Italian, but not a good Catholic. He only attended mass on holidays, but those little times in church pushed him to ask the question. I think he was secretly hoping it would be answered.

God answered my father's prayer rather quickly. Two weeks later my father encountered God in a real way. And it changed his life forever. My dad was making a commercial for the restaurant at a TV station in Dallas. He thought it would be funny to suggest they pray before the taping. The television station had recently turned to Christian programming. Pat Robertson, host of *The 700 Club*, owned the television station at the time.

To my father's surprise, everyone put down what they were doing and grabbed hands. Within a matter of seconds, he was holding hands with some man and praying. The whole station became quiet as prayers were lifted for the taping of the commercial. After my father's initial surprise, he said he felt a warm, electric feeling run up his hands and arms and all through his body. He couldn't forget it. Eventually it led to questions, and later he was led to a relationship with Jesus Christ by the station manager. My dad became a born-again Christian. Little did he know how many problems this would cause with his family and business. But my dad couldn't go back to his old life. He was changed.

One of the biggest attractions of the restaurant was the bar; it made the most money. The food and entertainment were outstanding, but the alcohol was what paid the bills. One day Pat Robertson (he mentored my dad) came into the restaurant to eat and asked my dad if he thought serving alcohol might be ruining his witness. My dad was confused. He didn't really understand what he meant by "witness." And he wasn't about to give up serving alcohol. Pat asked him to pray about it right then. How do you turn down Pat Robertson when he asks you to pray? Reluctantly, my father agreed. That was at lunch time.

Just a few hours later, my dad realized Pat was right. His bar was not a good witness. It was not glorifying God. Without any notice to my mom, my father stood on a chair in the bar and told everyone to go home. He was closing the bar. It made the local news. For months people in Dallas and elsewhere were talking about my father and the Italian Village restaurant. Everyone thought he had gone crazy when he gave up the coveted liquor license and sent it back to the state.

It was a horrible embarrassment to my dad's parents. There had already been a rift between my parents and grandparents. This was the final blow. My grandparents would no longer talk to my parents. My mom and dad tried to mend the fences, but Italians are difficult people to persuade. We were dead to them. We became estranged from the rest of the family and were eventually disowned. It was devastating to all of us. My parents never wanted it to end that way. My grandparents eventually died. The situation was left unresolved.

Leaving the Family

While I was in the hospital mulling over how to leave my family, I thought about how hard it would be on my parents. My oldest sister had already left the family several years earlier due to complications in their relationship. If I left, my middle sister would be the only daughter speaking to my parents. My parents would have to relive the nightmare a third time. It would bring up all the memories of their estrangement from my grandparents and my oldest sister. I knew it would be a lot for them to handle emotionally, but I felt my hand was forced. It took a life-threatening illness for me to make such a difficult decision.

I felt bad about leaving, but I was tired of living up to expectations I could no longer fulfill. And I was angry about unresolved issues between us. I didn't feel validated or heard when I asked for changes in our relationship over the years. Here I was in my 40s, a Christian woman who grew up in the church, leaving her family. I knew it would look bad. But I was happy. I bounced between fear, guilt, and sheer joy. I felt a huge burden lifted off my shoulders.

Little did I know I would trade one burden for another. Being estranged isn't all it is cracked up to be. I thought once I was free of my family, all the problems would go away. Instead, I traded them in for new ones. At the time, I didn't care. I was leaving my family, Christian or not.

Introspection

1. What is your family history?
2. Are you angry or bitter about your family?
3. Are you considering walking away or already estranged?
4. If you are suffering from a chronic illness, would you be willing to ask God if there is a connection?
5. Will you cry out to God and ask Him to help you with your situation?

Verses for Spiritual Warfare

Psalm 103:2-5
> Praise the Lord, my soul, and forget not all his benefits—who forgives all your sins and heals all your diseases, who redeems your life from the pit and crowns you with love and compassion, who satisfies your desires with good things so that your youth is renewed like the eagle's.

Psalm 34:18
> The Lord is close to the brokenhearted and saves those who are crushed in spirit.

2 Corinthians 12:9a
> But he said to me, "My grace is sufficient for you, for my power is made perfect in weakness."

Isaiah 41:10
> So do not fear, for I am with you; do not be dismayed, for I am your God. I will strengthen you and help you; I will uphold you with my righteous right hand.

Psalm 107:13
> Then they cried to the Lord in their trouble, and he saved them from their distress.

CHAPTER 2

Leaving a Christian Family

In 1977, my parents shut the doors of the Italian Village and changed professions. My father had no job offers other than to work at our church as a janitor. He took the job and made the best of it. He was very gifted at working with his hands, so it was a real blessing to the church and to us. God has a sense of humor, ex-millionaire turned janitor.

After a year, my dad was offered a position on staff. This is how he got into full-time ministry. And then the next year, when I was in sixth grade, my father became the associate pastor. The church exploded in size while we were there. It became a true megachurch. Over the span of my father's career, he pastored at four megachurches in the area. He served as associate pastor in two of the four churches.

Leaving my family was going to be more than just a little footnote. It would cause a lot of gossip and speculation among friends, since my father had been in ministry for 30 years. People would be curious about why a pastor's family would split, and two out of three daughters leave.

Some people would assume the very worst. I want to make it clear that I am grateful I never experienced sexual violence, though I'm sure there are many estranged adult children who are dealing with this very issue. Whether you have been physically, spiritually, mentally, emotionally, or sexually abused, we all get trapped in relational patterns we don't know how to leave. The good news is that family dysfunction didn't start with you. It started at the beginning of time.

Families in the Bible

Starting in Genesis 4, we see the breakdown of the first family. Cain killed his brother Abel. A couple chapters later, Noah got drunk, and his son, Ham, made a mockery of him, which had bad results for Ham and his children. Next, we have Lot. His daughters got him drunk, and each one had sex with him to produce an heir. The Moabites and the Ammonites were the direct result of those incestuous relationships.

The Bible then highlights the sinful deception of Jacob, who deceived his brother Esau with the help of his mother. There was also a sister rivalry. Rachel and Leah, who were both married to Jacob, hated each other. There was a constant competition between them. Samuel 8 tells the story of Samuel, a priest in ministry, who had two sons who took bribes and perverted justice. It was because of these two ungodly men that the Israelites asked for a king. That didn't work out so well.

Israel's first king, Saul, hurled a spear at his son, Jonathan, and tried to kill him. The next king, David, had a newborn child who died because of his adultery. One of his other sons, Absalom, killed his half-brother, Amnon, for raping his sister, Tamar. Then he tried to kill King David and take over the throne. The Bible sometimes reads like a true soap opera. Your problems are not new. Family problems have been going on since the beginning of time.

My Family Dysfunction

My own family dysfunction was, in fact, a cycle of unhealthy relational patterns. Enough to have two generations of estrangements. More law than grace was demonstrated. A severity that was unbearable for me and my husband. Like many families, my family failed to communicate well. When we did communicate, we often said hurtful things without thought. We harbored anger and bitterness, and we struggled with pride and unforgiveness. Everyone had unmet expectations. There was a tendency to either make ultimatums or run away when problems became too difficult to work through.

In my opinion, the problem with my family was we got stuck at ground zero. We could never agree on something as simple as what the problems were, or their root causes because we didn't talk. Since no one took ownership, there was no way to move forward and address who or what needed to change. Once the family started splitting, we could not untangle the mess. The situation became so convoluted we couldn't even verbalize what really happened or how to fix it. It was just the way things were.

The exact details of my family split don't really matter; it is not the focus of this book. This book focuses on how God rescued us from ourselves and brought us back to a place of forgiveness. It is about Jesus and what He did in my family. Not what we did or didn't do.

What I am most grateful for is that my parents decided to follow Christ many years ago. I may have never become a Christian if it weren't for them. As a family who has been in ministry, we rejoice in sharing our journey with others so they may see God's glory in our pain.

Families in Ministry

Growing up, I thought Christian families who worked in ministry should be perfect. I think we all did. We came across as flawless. Looking from the outside, people saw that my sisters and I were high achievers, social, well liked, and were following God. But internally, there was a lot of pressure to look good, since we were in the spotlight 24/7. I didn't want to be the one to crack that image and ruin the perception. That kind of pressure is a lot for a kid.

When families in ministry do hit a crisis, many times it gets quietly swept under the rug in hopes that the problems will eventually go away, and no one will know about them. I suspect my family is not the only one who has struggled in this area. There is a natural tendency to hide things no matter who you are. It is a difficult balance to know when to be transparent and get help or muddle through on your own. The issue with muddling through is that big problems don't just go away. You can only stay in denial for so long until it comes out in some other form or fashion. It may come out overtly in the form of yelling, fighting, tantrums, domination, or threats. Or it could come out covertly in the form of health issues, retribution, self-hate, suicidal tendencies, backstabbing, gossip, etc.

One way or another, you eventually deal with the problems. For me, it came out in my health issues. I could no longer hide my pain. I wanted to deal with our family directly—address things head on and make changes. I didn't like the way we interacted with each other. Our relationship felt unbalanced. I wanted a relationship where we respected each other as equals. But it was too hard for our family patterns to be broken. Over the years, any suggestions I made were not heard or just not understood.

It is easy to get stuck as a family. Deep down I knew my family had issues, but I didn't know what to do to bring about healthier interactions. I was forced to sweep it under the rug. I kept hoping somehow things would change. I prayed for God to intervene. I was disappointed and angry He didn't miraculously alter the dynamics of our family. I didn't realize we had to make the time and be willing to do the work.

As Christians, we can be working for God's kingdom doing really good things and not realize there are problems with our own family. We were all busy with church, activities, school, and life. It happened slowly over time. We were so busy helping others, yet we didn't realize we needed to help ourselves. By the time we realized we needed help, it was too late.

Family Counseling

We tried family counseling after the split. It was a disaster. There were so many unresolved issues. There was too much anger on all sides. Each of us needed our space. We had to wait and let the Holy Spirit work on us. It was the best route for our family at the time. Again, leaving wasn't my first choice. I felt forced because of my health.

Family counseling may be an option that you and your family decide to try. Many times, it can help. Realize there are a few nuances. All parties must be willing to invest time and emotional energy, they must be physically healthy, and they must have enough money just to begin counseling. This may not always be feasible. Once in counseling, it is easy to quit when it gets painful. Most of all, you pray your counselor is good at his job. If not, it can actually make things worse.

When you go to a counselor as a family for a long period of time, there is a chance everyone will get angrier. It can make the split even more pronounced. My husband and I were steadfast in our decision to remain estranged from my family after the counselor came into the picture. In our case, we were angrier after the counseling experience. And so were my parents.

Perhaps you won't be in the same pickle if you see the warning signs sooner. The trick is to recognize the problems and deal with them earlier rather than later, so that you are not pushed into a corner like we were. If I could do it over, I would try a mediator instead of a counselor. Having everyone in separate rooms with a mediator going to each room would have been quicker, and things would not have gotten lost in translation over time. It would have taken a day to figure out whether we could work through things or not. Meeting together at one time and having us in different rooms would have been better than several months of raw emotions, miscommunication, and, eventually, retaliation.

You have a choice when you see this happening in your family. You can either choose to address the problems and change or not. The problems in my family stayed unresolved. No one was willing to budge after a counselor got involved. The problems escalated until the rift was so bad there became a gulf between us. The relationship had been declining for years. Leaving just made it official.

Introspection

1. Are you ignoring family issues that need to be resolved?
2. Will you seek God for help and ask Him to show you what you have done inappropriately?
3. Will you go back and resolve the issues with each family member in a heart of humility?
4. If you are stuck, will you seek godly guidance from a counselor, pastor, or a mediator?
5. Will you do whatever it takes to get your part right before it is too late?

Verses for Spiritual Warfare

Ephesians 4:2
  Be completely humble and gentle; be patient, bearing one another in love.

James 4:6
  But he gives us more grace. That is why Scripture says: "God opposes the proud but shows favor to the humble."

Colossians 3:12
  Therefore, as God's chosen people, holy and dearly loved, clothe yourselves with compassion, kindness, humility, gentleness and patience.

Jeremiah 33:3
  "Call to me and I will answer you and tell you great and unsearchable things you do not know."

Proverbs 21:2
  A person may think their own ways are right, but the Lord weighs the heart.

CHAPTER 3

Estranged from Family

In October of 2009, about a year after that fateful day in the hospital, I walked away from my extended family. I had a heated discussion with my mother and told her how I really felt about the dynamics of our relationship. Although what I said was true, it was not well received because of my angry tone. I had set boundaries in our relationship and felt my mother and my father were not adhering to them. I decided leaving was the best way to get their attention, so I said the "right things" that would effectively end our relationship. (We all know how to push the "big buttons.")

I was trying to tell my mother I wanted to be respected as an adult. I didn't hold anything back during this conversation. I knew it was aggressive, but I didn't care. It would have been better if we had been talking through things all along, but I never felt the freedom to do that with my parents. I wanted to be heard.

Since our relationship was already hanging by a thread, I knew there was nothing to stop me from telling her how I really felt. I didn't care if my mom was angry. In fact, I hoped she was angry. I wanted her to feel my pain. That volcanic eruption on the phone was the last conversation I had with her for seven years. I never thought the silence would last that long. Time just kept passing. Year after year went by, and no one talked. I thought if I left, my parents would change immediately. And then I would come back. I was wrong.

That's the problem with estrangement. Once you walk away, you are no longer in control of how long it will last. If no one is talking, there is never any hope of reconciliation. Each person stays on his or her side of the line. No one budges, because each side is waiting for an apology. And then the years go by with no communication. Here is what happened during those seven years, starting in October of 2009.

YEAR ONE: 2009-2010
Health Regained

The first year, I was relieved to be away from my family. I was glad to have the time to decompress. I started working on the fear and anger during my prayer times. You may be shocked I was praying. But I was. I never wanted to leave my faith. I just wanted to leave my family for a while. Thank heavens God didn't leave me. God wrapped Himself around me during that time and showed me what His love looked like when I felt unlovable. He came after me and never let me go.

Some of you may have decided you can't be a Christian and leave. Perhaps you believe that a real Christian wouldn't choose estrangement. It certainly wasn't my first choice, but God was big enough to use it for His glory. For me, the breakdown was with my family, not with God. I actually left so I could get healing. Not only physically, but mentally, spiritually, and emotionally.

I needed to find out who I was and what I really believed about God and His love. Oddly enough, I had to come to my own faith. Even though I was a believer and grew up in the church, I didn't really know who I was as a Christian. I needed to look to God and no one else. I realized I was spending more time trying to please my parents and others than trying to please God. I was a high achiever and had built my life on performance and perfectionism. I thrived on being a perfect Christian, a perfect student, perfect wife/mother, and a perfect daughter. I found this model to be unsustainable. I couldn't do it all.

Getting away helped me to regain the ability to eat. I slowly began to digest my food, and my weight returned to normal. After that year, I could eat whatever I wanted. I was no longer in jeopardy of losing my colon. I was in more of a management phase. Throughout the year, I thought about the situation over and over again, wondering what I could have done differently. It was always the same conclusion. Nothing. There was nothing I could have done to change the situation.

I felt guilt and shame for leaving, but I was getting well physically, so I knew it had been my only real choice if I'd wanted to change my diagnosis. All of these feelings were like a big bowl of spaghetti mixed up in my head. I didn't know how to untangle the mess.

YEAR TWO: 2010-2011
Counseling

After a year of obsessing about the situation, I decided to go to a counselor alone. Estrangement was bad for my soul. I wanted a way back to inner peace. I had no control over anyone but myself, so that is what I did—I worked on me. Counseling helped me tremendously. I was able to unravel some of the lies I was telling myself. And I gained some tools to help me deal with the conflict. Here are some of the lies I had been telling myself. Are you telling yourself these same things?

- It is all my fault.
- It is all their fault.
- No one can really love me—not even my parents.
- I am not worthy of love.
- I am abandoned.
- No one understands me.

- I am a failure.
- I am embarrassed.
- God doesn't understand or care.
- God is going to leave me since I am estranged.
- I am broken.
- This will never get fixed.
- I will always be afraid.
- I'll never stop being angry.
- I can't forgive.
- I am alone.

After I acknowledged that these were lies, I began combatting them with truth from God's word. I started making notecards with Scripture and words of truth on them. I got the idea from Beth Moore. She called it "re-wallpapering" your mind. Each day I read those cards and reprogrammed my brain to believe something different. I figured if it worked for her, it could work for me.

I didn't believe the cards at first. It took time. I figured if it came out of the Bible, then I could ask God to help me believe it. Over time, it started resonating in my spirit. After a while, I realized this truth was medicine for my soul. I wanted more and more. I still have to remind myself of the truth. It is something I will have to do the rest of my life. (Even if you don't reconcile, it is important to do this for your own health.)

Also, during this year I prayed that God would show me what His love looked like. This prayer was answered immediately. Everywhere I turned there was someone talking about God's love. Our sermon series at church was about love. Our Sunday school series for the year? God's love. I turned on Christian radio—God's love. It was so startling that I just had to laugh. God figured out how to reach me in some interesting ways. I found that God didn't just love everyone else. He loved me too. He loved me enough to chase me. What a difference that made for me. I rebuilt my foundation with God's love.

In her book *Praying God's Word*, Beth Moore quotes Dennis Jernigan:[1]

> True freedom will only bloom in your life when you put on the truth of who God says you are. Knowing who God wants you to be is not the same as practicing who He wants you to be. When life gets complicated and failures abound, turn your heart back to the basics. Remember who you are in Christ, practice being who God says you are, and in time, you will be walking in the . . . hall of freedom.

---

[1] Moore, Beth. *Praying Gods Word: Breaking Free from Spiritual Strongholds.* B&H Publishing Group, 2018, p. 87.

YEAR THREE: 2011-2012
The Heart Attack

My dad had a heart attack. My middle sister, who was not estranged from them, called me and told me about it. It was serious. There was a chance my dad would not make it through surgery. After talking and praying about it with my husband, we decided to go see him. I was terrified. My stomach was in knots. My hands were sweaty, and my heart was beating out of my chest.

I wasn't sure how my dad would react when I showed up. When I walked down the hall of the hospital to his room, I became paralyzed. I stopped in the hall next to his room. I had second thoughts. I couldn't do it. I felt like if I went to see him, I was saying everything that happened was okay. That there were no problems or that we could sweep them all under the rug again.

Something inside of me told me to keep going to his room. It would be okay. The Holy Spirit was there pressing me to see my dad. I obeyed. To my surprise, my father was very kind. We made small talk and only stayed for about 15 minutes. Nothing really happened after that meeting, but God showed me that I could have some sort of relationship with my parents in the future.

I didn't feel all the old anger when I saw my dad. I looked at my father as just another person. He wasn't so scary lying in a hospital bed connected to all those wires. I thought for sure my parents would call and apologize after I came to the hospital. Nothing happened. I was confused. Years later my mother told me she was wondering when we were going to call and apologize. None of us thought we were in the wrong. We clearly needed more time.

YEAR FOUR: 2012-2013
Nothing

It was a lot of nothing. I wish I could say something happened, but it didn't. I kept praying and asking God to move in my family. I was learning to trust Him even when I couldn't see any movement toward reconciliation. I had many moments of doubt and anger. I wanted God to act.

YEAR FIVE: 2013-2014
Nothing Again

Waiting. More waiting. Praying, begging, and wondering where God was in the whole situation. I kept working on myself and practicing everything I learned in counseling. I really struggled with God being silent. I felt abandoned. It felt like he was not listening. His silence was deafening. I felt completely alone.

YEAR SIX: 2014-2015
Disaster

This was the worst year of my life. I began to see the curse of estrangement being passed down to the next generation. I was slowly walking into another relationship break, only this time it was with my child. I have never cried so much in my life. I couldn't stop what was set into motion. I felt completely out of control. I saw my child slowly slipping through my hands and falling into another world that did not include me or our family values.

As a Christian, I had to believe that what we taught our child from birth would not return void. I constantly reminded myself of Proverbs 22:6: "Start children off on the way they should go, and even when they are old, they will not turn from it." There was nothing else left to do but run to God again. And pray.

YEAR SEVEN: 2015-2016
Prayer

This is when I really learned how to pray. I had bought *The Power of a Praying Parent* by Stormie Omartian years earlier. At the end of every chapter, there is a specific prayer to pray. I would pick out a couple of prayers and pray them for my kids occasionally. The prayers helped me to know the truth and to hone in on specific issues of concern. But when my child started acting out, I took every prayer in the book and prayed them every day. I was desperate. I was worried my child would never feel anything but anger toward my husband and me.

I started to understand how my parents must have felt about me. You are heartbroken and angry all at once. It was a roller coaster of emotions. It took a while, but my child finally started talking to us about the problems. My husband and I felt like we needed to do everything we could to make things right with our child. With the help of a counselor, we worked on changing a few things. We didn't do anything to compromise our values, but we learned ways to handle problems a little better. Today, we have a wonderful relationship with both of our adult children. I know it is because we prayed for wisdom and interceded on their behalf daily. I believe it made all the difference.

What I learned from this situation is prayer is powerful. As a believer, I knew this because I heard it in church all the time. But you don't really understand it until there is a big problem in your life. This was the year I made the jump from hearing to doing. I then began to pray with the same kind of passion and fervency for my entire family as I had prayed for my child.

I seriously started praying for my parents in November of 2016. I didn't want to spend another Christmas without them. I asked God to let that year be the last holiday I would be estranged. It was then I knew I wanted to go back.

I prayed for God to make a way. It was like walking down a dark hallway. I couldn't see any light, but I knew Jesus was the light. I had to trust in that alone.

YEAR EIGHT: JANUARY 2017
Reconciliation

I had no idea this would be the year we would reconcile. I was losing faith that there would ever be any changes. It was at this point that I added fasting to my prayers. That's when things changed. My counselor said there was 99% chance things would never change. God did come through in a mighty way. There were eight miracles that happened exactly in a one-year time period. I didn't even recognize all the miracles until I wrote this book.

In chapter eight I will go into all the details. Every time I think about what happened, I am amazed that God came through in such a miraculous way. God heard all of our cries to Him. Not just my cries, but also those of my parents and others in our family. If God can do this for my family, He can do it for yours. Just don't get too set on the way you think God should go about things. You have to be willing to let Him move in His way and in His time. We all had to be flexible, because the way it all happened can only be explained as divine intervention. I had to be willing to put down all my anger and not retaliate.

Introspection

1. Do you struggle with accepting God's love?
2. Are you telling yourself lies?
3. If you are believing lies, will you start reprogramming yourself with the truth?
4. If you struggle with trusting God, will you reach out to Him and ask Him to help you in this area?
5. Will you walk in obedience to what He is calling you to do?

Verses for Spiritual Warfare

Romans 8:35, 37-39
> Who shall separate us from the love of Christ? Shall trouble or hardship or persecution or famine or nakedness or danger or sword? No, in all these things we are more than conquerors through him who loved us. For I am convinced that neither death nor life, neither angels nor demons, neither the present nor the future, nor any powers, neither height nor depth, not anything else in all creation, will be able to separate us from the love of God that is in Christ Jesus our Lord.

1 Peter 1:22
> Now that you have purified yourselves by obeying the truth so that you have sincere love for each other, love one another deeply, from the heart.

2 Corinthians 4:2
> Rather, we have renounced secret and shameful ways; we do not use deception, nor do we distort the word of God. On the contrary, by setting forth the truth plainly we commend ourselves to everyone's conscience in the sight of God.

John 8:32
> Then you will know the truth, and the truth will set you free.

CHAPTER 4

Retaliation Never Works

In the last chapter, I mentioned how I unloaded on my mother. I had so much anger pent up that I said too many things at one time. It was so forceful that she couldn't hear the message. At that point, I didn't really care. I was going to give my final thoughts whether she wanted to hear them or not.

We all have things we know will "get" our family members. Things we know will cause an incredible amount of anger and hurt. I was purposely trying to break the relationship with my mother, because I didn't like the way we interacted with each other. I couldn't figure out how to restructure it so we could relate to each other as equals. I tried telling her over the years, but I don't think she really understood.

If you find yourself in a similar situation as the parent, there is a fork in the road. You can choose to be furious, or you can recognize it for what it is. Your adult child is trying to tell you, "We need to change the way we do things in our relationship." I didn't know how else to say this to my mom and dad. I wanted some changes in our relationship. I didn't feel heard. They heard me after that.

Often adult children do articulate the problem before they leave. For some reason, there is a disconnect between the parents and the adult child. The parents are actually dumbfounded when the child does leave the family, not really knowing what went wrong. They may even maintain they were never told about the problems.

The adult child is shocked the parents don't understand the problems, especially after multiple heated conversations. This is a clear sign that the communication has broken down between the generations. It is as if there are two different realities. Each side is blinded from seeing the other's point of view.

One of the problems in my family was that my parents expected me to come to their world and participate in their lives. I had been doing that for most of my life. I no longer wanted to do that. I wanted them to come to my world and participate in my life and in my kids' lives. I was expecting them to go to my kids' games, know my friends, help with babysitting, etc.

My parents wanted me to be involved with their interests, help put up their Christmas decorations, know their friends, take care of their pets, run their errands, etc. We had very different ideas and expectations about how we were supposed to participate in each other's lives. And we were all angry when our needs were not met. Both sides felt unloved and ignored.

What Next?

You can respond with retaliation when there are heated discussions, or you can stop the escalation and listen. Listen to what the other person is saying. Resist the urge to retaliate. It will be difficult, but it may save what little relationship is left. If one retaliates, chances are the other will respond in kind. And then it snowballs. Here are some sinful responses I have seen happen in families when adult children leave:

- Rude messages sent between family members
- Lawsuits between family members
- Suicidal tendencies
- Threats regarding the will or disownment
- Revoking or severely restricting relationships with the grandchildren
- Physical and verbal threats
- Rumors and gossip created in the community
- Family members used as pawns
- Family members forced to choose sides
- Bribes
- Attempts to control with money

- Dramatic displays of emotion to invoke pity
- Shaming tactics

I am sure there are more, but these are a few I have seen or heard about over the years when families are in crisis. I realize sometimes we have to set severe boundaries when they have been overstepped in the past. It may even be necessary for protection until there is real change. It is important to examine your heart before exercising any restrictions, so they are not used simply as retribution.

I don't know why we think punishment or retribution is going to help the situation. Just reading the above list aloud, most sane people would agree these are not productive behaviors. Yet, sadly, we see this kind of reaction within Christian families. We should know better, but we are sinful humans. We start acting in the flesh. No one is walking in the Spirit at this point. We try to save face because our pride is hurt.

We don't act any different from unbelievers when we behave this way. And then we become embarrassed, because we can't explain this to our Christian friends. We know this is not Christ-like behavior, but at this point, things have sunk to a new low. There is no going back. When the dust settles, everyone looks around at the collateral damage. No one has won. It is like the Gingham Dog and the Calico Cat. Both sides have devoured each other. It has become so clouded by all the threats. Now you have not only the original problem that existed, but also all the escalation tactics that have muddied the water exponentially.

Sometimes the retaliation is actually worse than the original problem. This makes it ten times harder to forgive. Once the water is poisoned, it is hard to go back and clean up what was said or done. If you are in the mode of retaliation, stop. It will only make things worse. Everyone loses. Take a moment to breathe. Let everyone cool down. Examine your behavior and ask God if you have done anything displeasing to Him. If you have behaved badly, apologize now.

Time is not on your side when there is an estrangement. It is easy to get a hard heart when things are left unresolved. This is where I went so terribly wrong. I simmered, stewed, and didn't forgive easily. I obsessed about the wrongs done to me. An alternative is to set tighter boundaries and step back. You can make apologies, forgive and not have a close relationship. See if the tighter boundaries will be respected. When I talk to people about their family issues, I try to recommend this option first. I also recommend prayer. More prayer than ever before. I have seen more things accomplished by the unseen rather than the seen.

Sometimes just letting a bit of time pass can help everyone come back with cooler heads. And then other times, it doesn't matter what you do. Boundaries are broken, and the same behavior repeats itself year after year. When this continues to happen, you have a difficult decision to make.

Before you decide to cut bait all together, it is good to examine the cost of leaving. Having a distant relationship may be better than a full-out estrangement. There is a high cost when you leave the family. You may not realize it at the time. This one decision has a ripple effect for generations. It is hard to cross back over the chasm once it is in place. I am living proof that it is possible to come back, but it is difficult. Before you leave, I want to give you a look into your future and help you better understand the consequences of estrangement.

Introspection

1. Are you retaliating in any way?
2. If you are retaliating, is it helping?
3. Is there anything positive you could do instead of retaliating?
4. Will you replace your retaliation with prayer?
5. Will you release the situation to God?

Verses for Spiritual Warfare

1 Peter 3:9
   Do not repay evil with evil or insult with insult. On the contrary, repay evil with blessing, because to this you were called so that you may inherit a blessing.

Proverbs 24:29
   Do not say, "I'll do to them as they have done to me; I'll pay them back for what they did."

Proverbs 15:18
   A hot-tempered person stirs up conflict, but the one who is patient calms a quarrel.

Proverbs 12:16
   Fools show their annoyance at once, but the prudent overlook an insult.

Proverbs 10:23
   A fool finds pleasure in wicked schemes, but a person of understanding delights in wisdom.

Proverbs 24:3
   By wisdom a house is built, and through understanding it is established.

CHAPTER 5

The Consequences of Estrangement

Seven years was a long time to be estranged from my family. Breaking away from them completely was definitely not my first choice. I do not believe it is God's first choice either. Unfortunately, sometimes it is necessary for everyone to step away from each other to find peace. In my specific case, I felt forced because of my health.

If you are considering breaking away from your family, first of all, I am sorry you are even at this juncture in your life. It is a horrible decision and not one to be taken lightly. Second, I ask you to count the cost. Consider what is at stake if you do not choose to work it out by talking to each other or getting outside help. Leaving may be what you want, but it is good to think about it before you make that choice. Whatever you do, choose carefully. Meeting with a counselor or a mediator is painful, but estrangement has its own pain. There is no get-out-of-jail-free card.

The longer you are away, the wider the gap becomes. Feelings become entrenched, and lines in the sand are drawn forever. Each party thinks the other side is wrong and needs to apologize. Though I didn't account for them at the time of my decision, being estranged proved to have some trade-offs. I didn't realize how it would affect everyone else in the family. All of us suffered in different ways because of the family break. Here are five common consequences when family members stop talking to one another:

1. Lost Time

When you break relationships, you lose precious time. My kids lost their grandparents at a crucial point in their lives. My son was 15 years old (9th grade), and my daughter was 11 years old (5th grade). When we reconciled, my son was 22 and a senior in college. My daughter was 18 and a senior in high school.

This time can never be regained.

My kids were both growing and changing so much when we left. When we did return, my parents didn't even recognize them. Both of my kids had become adults during the seven years we were gone. Now that my kids are adults, they are busy. It is hard for them to make the time to see their grandparents. They have moved on with their lives. Neither of them lives in Texas at the moment. Those crucial years of relationship development were missed. They may never be close with my parents now.

2. Lost Resources

When your family stops talking, you lose resources. Wisdom could have been pooled together. If my parents and I had resolved our differences sooner, they could have been there for me when things were hard with my own children. Kids can be an enigma at times. Having the experience of your parents helps—they were raising you not too long ago. They remember a few things.

Another benefit of going to your parents for advice is that you often don't have to spend a lot of time filling in details. They already know some context. Not having that resource was more difficult than I ever thought it would be. There were days I wanted to call my mom so badly and ask her about parenting a teenager. Instead, I had no one to call and ask for help.

3. Lost Extended Family Connections

When your family stops talking, you lose extended family connections too. We not only lost my parents, but we all also lost aunts, uncles, and cousins. It was a ripple effect. There were seven years' worth of holidays, birthdays, weddings, and anniversaries we missed participating in as a family. We missed my niece's wedding, which was really hard. I can never go back and experience that event.

It gets messy when someone gets married, has a baby, has a birthday, or hosts a holiday gathering. Some get uninvited, and others won't come if certain people are going to be there. More feelings get hurt. It puts everyone in an awkward position, because someone is always left out. No one means to keep from including others, but choices must be made in the end. And that person remembers being left out, causing a new strain between another group of family members. Hurt feelings cause more hurt feelings. Negative emotions toward family members multiply with a family split. It is like a virus. It infects everyone. And everyone feels powerless to make it go away.

Holidays were especially hard. It is nice to have a place to go and to be with the people who love you the most. (Unless your family fights when you're all together.) We always had my husband's side of the family over for the holidays, but it was quiet after that. My side of the family was missing. There are over a dozen people in my family who get together from time to time. It was lonely and depressing not seeing them.

I wasn't the only one suffering; it hurt my kids too. They missed seeing their eight cousins together at one time. This used to be one of their favorite things to do as a family. The five boys would play football and video games, and the five girls would get together to talk and watch movies. Sometimes, there would be sleepovers at my parents' house, since they could accommodate large groups.

All of that went away after my sister and I left. Leaving shattered the connection my kids had with some of their cousins. Nothing was ever the same. Now all of the cousins are adults. It is next to impossible to get us all together on the same day. Some of my nieces and nephews are now married and have moved away. Many of them celebrate the holidays at home with their own kids.

Some children may not realize they are estranged when they are forced to choose one family member over another and have limited contact. They never meant to leave the family, but it happened due to strained relationships from their parents. This is how it carries from one generation to another generation.

4. Shame

When your family stops talking, you feel shame. I was embarrassed to tell people my secret. Or if I did, I felt the need to explain it. I never could exactly explain it, because I didn't even know what happened. It was déjà vu. If you recall from the first chapter, the estrangement started with my grandparents. And then my oldest sister left the family when she became an adult. I had already spent years explaining those estrangements, and now I was explaining my own estrangement from my parents.

My kids had to explain the situation to their friends and people they dated. They were embarrassed too. It was messy. No one really knew how to handle it or even what to say. There is no etiquette for family estrangement.

5. A Generational Curse

When your family stops talking, you set in motion a possible generational curse. The sins of the father are passed down to the next generation. Numbers 14:18 says, "The Lord is slow to anger, abounding in love and forgiving sin and rebellion. Yet he does not leave the guilty unpunished; he punishes the children for the sin of the parents to the third and fourth generation." There had already been breaks in two generations. I wanted it to stop. I didn't want to contribute to the problem, if at all possible. I certainly didn't want to give Satan an opportunity to gain a foothold in my own family. I wanted to show my kids I could work things out. And so could they.

I would like to point out there are parents who will try to use this scripture as a form of manipulation to lure an adult child back into a toxic family system where no real change has taken place. I believe the root of generational curses start with unforgiveness. Whether you return or not, you need to forgive completely, and prayerfully consider whether you are returning into a safe environment. One needs to return into a loving and respectful relationship, so abuse does not repeat itself.

Before Your Family Stops Talking

It is important to count the cost before you totally break off relationships. Instead, try to step back. Take a breather. If you are not talking, things will NEVER get worked out. Learn how to set boundaries, work on forgiveness, and see if you can find solutions that work for everyone. Whatever you do, pray before moving in a certain direction.

Being on the other side of estrangement, I can say that it was the right thing for me to leave. But the interim was horrible in its own way. So many people suffered in the process. I didn't account for that. God has used it for good, but I wish there had been an easier way for my family to find some middle ground and deal with the real problems.

Introspection

1. Will you consider the ramifications before you leave your family?
2. Will you try setting firmer boundaries and sticking to them before you decide to leave?
3. Will you approach the person offending you one more time?
4. Will you forgive, even if the other person has clearly wronged you?
5. Will you pray for God to show you creative ways to handle the situation?

Verses for Spiritual Warfare

James 1:5
> If any of you lacks wisdom, you should ask God, who gives generously to all without finding fault, and it will be given to him.

Psalm 32:8
> I will instruct you and teach you in the way you should go; I will counsel you with my loving eye on you.

James 1:19-20
> My dear brothers and sisters, take note of this: Everyone should be quick to listen, slow to speak and slow to become angry, because human anger does not produce the righteousness that God desires.

Matthew 5:23-24
> Therefore, if you are offering your gift at the altar and there remember that your brother or sister has something against you, leave your gift there in front of the altar. First go and be reconciled to them; then come and offer your gift.

Proverbs 3:13-14
> Blessed are those who find wisdom, those who gain understanding, for she is more profitable than silver and yields better returns than gold.

CHAPTER 6

The Real Problem with Families

I have listened to many women tell me about their family issues, and I have read dozens more online accounts from women who are desperately seeking help. They all have different stories, each one uniquely painful and heartbreaking. It is hard to find the common thread in each story. I want so badly to pinpoint the real problem. It would be nice to say, "Here is the problem, so do such-and-such and everything will be fine." Unfortunately, it is rarely that simple.

Family rifts and estrangements are complicated. I can't begin to list all the reasons families break apart, but there do seem to be a few recurring themes. As you are reading through the list, consider your own family. Ask yourself what part you or other members may be playing. Carefully examine whether you are participating in some of these destructive behaviors.

Addiction

Adult children and parents can get caught in the terrible trap of addiction. This is not something that is just going on with non-Christians. It is happening in many Christian homes as well—even within families in full-time ministry. Addiction is no respecter of faith. It insidiously slips into families no matter what they believe.

One of my closest childhood friends died at the age of 40 from a heart attack. She had been abusing prescription drugs for years. The prescription addiction started after an injury. She needed it for the pain, but eventually got hooked. It was medicating her emotional pain too. My friend came from a well-known Christian family. The family was highly dysfunctional in so many ways.

My friend was raised by her grandparents, because the parents could not handle the responsibility. She did have a relationship with her mother when she was older, but it was strained. There were a few core issues they could never resolve. The obvious issue was abandonment. I watched my friend suffer tremendously because of how her family acted behind closed doors. There were family secrets that would repulse any person, Christian or not. She used prescription medication to escape the pain of her childhood traumas, and it eventually led to her death.

I strongly encourage you to assess your behavior. You could be suffering from an addiction and not even realize it.

If you are caught in this trap, it is likely this is playing a huge part in your family issues. Your addiction is controlling who you are as a person and how you behave. You may not think your behavior is hurting other people, but it is. The time you are spending with your addiction is taking away from those who love you. And who you are as a person is dramatically altered from the real you. Maybe you don't like the real you, and this is why you have an addiction. All the more reason to get help!

Mental Illness

Mental illness or personality disorder is another common factor in broken families. Families don't know what to do to help their loved one. They have no idea why the person acts a certain way. Sometimes they're convinced it is just the person's character, because he or she has always been this way.

Diagnosis is hard, whether it is the parent or the adult child with the mental illness, since both parties are of age. It can get swept under the rug, while everyone is left trying to simply get by. After many years of dealing with the same problem, family members are fed up with the bad behavior. They just want to get away from the offender. It may take an intervention from the family to get proper help. The trick is to know whether the person with the mental illness is willing to receive help.

Abuse

Abuse can come in many shapes and forms. Each type of abuse—physical, mental, spiritual, emotional, sexual, etc.—can cause a whole host of problems. None of us are perfect. Sometimes we raise our voices, say the wrong thing, or do something we regret. That is not what I am talking about. I am talking about the kind of abuse that goes on for years without any change. Some markers to look for are the following: dominance, control, manipulation, and/or threats.

This kind of behavior can be exhibited by the parent or the adult child. In many cases, the abuser will deny this is happening and actually blame the victim. (It can make a person feel crazy.) Other times, an abuser will express shame or guilt but will not move toward real change. Either behavior can do an enormous amount of damage. A licensed counselor can help diagnose the actual problems in a dysfunctional family. I suggest going to your own counselor as opposed to the whole family going to the same counselor. When everyone goes to the same counselor, private information gets passed around unintentionally. Whatever the abuse looks like, it tends to tear families apart, especially if there is no real healing or change.

Economic Control

Many times, parents will use money to keep their adult children within their sphere. It is a way to still have a line into their lives and control them. I realize there are many people who have family businesses. It can be done, but just know that you have to work really hard to keep the relationships healthy.

Behind closed doors, people practice a lot of the escalation tactics I mentioned in chapter four. They are so entangled financially they don't know where the family starts and the business ends. It's all tied up together. When money is involved, people tend to act differently. Whether parents are supporting their adult children, or they are in a family business together, the lines can become blurred quickly. The financial relationship may even begin to take precedence.

This happened with Abram and Lot in Genesis 13. Abram's flocks and Lot's flocks had become so big that they had to separate. There was infighting among the family and the herders. Abram was wise in the way he solved the problem with his family. He realized the relationship was more important than the stuff. Genesis 13:9 says, "So, Abram said to Lot, 'Let's not have any quarreling between you and me, or between your herders and mine, for we are close relatives.'"

Abram let Lot choose which way he wanted to go when they separated. Abram was older and had more, yet he deferred to Lot, who was younger and had less. Lot chose the good pasture and left Abram with the desert land. Abram knew Lot was choosing what seemed to be the better land. It was green and lush, while Abram was left with the desert sand.

Abram let Lot go without punishment, retribution, or resentment. Abram was more concerned about their relationship than anything else. He was older and wiser; he knew better. Unfortunately, the rest of the story doesn't turn out so well for Lot. Lot chose Sodom and Gomorrah, and, eventually, he lost everything. Despite all the conflict, Abram prayed for God to save Lot and his family. God listened. I am sure it must have been painful for Abram to watch Lot lose everything, but he loved him just the same.

Be willing to release your children even if you know they may not be making the right choices financially. Once your adult children leave home, they are in God's hands. They have their own fields to plow. Let them earn their own living. I understand it may be painful to watch. But you can accomplish more by praying to God, like Abram did, than trying to manipulate adult children and control them with your money (or the promise of future money). The relationship is more important than stuff.

Holiday Stress

Several years ago, my husband and I went through a class at our church for married couples. It is a Bible study curriculum specifically geared toward couples who want to enhance their marriages. Once a week, couples would meet for a time of lecture and then break up into small groups for discussion. In our group discussion, we heard a lot of things about each other's families. The one thing couples were struggling with the most was how to spend time during the holidays.

Many young couples felt forced to be at everyone's home on a certain day, but they also wanted to be in their own home. They wanted to create their own family traditions. It was especially difficult for parents with young children. I was horrified at some of the stories these young parents were telling. They would travel and see three sets of families on Christmas Day. It was a nightmare. By the end of the day, they had eaten three large meals and their kids were a crying mess.

The parents were frazzled trying to keep their kids from misbehaving at the relatives' homes. They felt a lot of pressure to make a good impression, since they didn't see everyone often. It had become such a problem that it was now causing issues in their marriage. The fighting would start weeks before the holiday and go on for days after the holiday was over. They were more concerned about the relatives being happy than taking care of their own family's needs.

The young parents were afraid to speak up to their extended family and tell them they were miserable. They were worried it would cause a rift within their family. Eventually the young families dreaded the holidays. They wanted to stay in their own home and enjoy a day of fun with their little kids. I can't say I blame them. There needed to be a balance.

We encouraged the young couples to set some boundaries with their relatives. It is important to find times that are good for everyone in the family, including the little kids.

Some relatives may be upset, but people-pleasing eventually causes a lot of resentment too. Most adult children just want to be loved and accepted by their parents and to have fun with them when they get together—whenever that is. Make it easy for everyone and accommodate the whole family. Healthy families adjust and compromise. They think about the good of everyone, not just their own demands. Parents need to have an open-door policy. Kids need to be free to come and go whenever they want, within reason.

Parental Alienation

Parental alienation is when a child is forced to break a relationship with another family member due to the adults not getting along. In the case of my family, it happened to me and my sisters when my parent's relationship broke with my grandparents, and it happened to my children when my husband and I became estranged from my family. In both cases, the family break immediately moved to the next generation when the relationship failed. I could no longer visit my grandparents when I was a child, and my kids could no longer visit my parents (their grandparents) when we left. Unfortunately, estrangement means the child is forced to take sides, sometimes for life, even though he had nothing to do with the relationship breakdown.

Dr. Deborah Newman says, "Some children may not think they are estranged because they have limited contact with a parent after the divorce. The child may not feel he made a conscious decision not to have a relationship with one parent because in his heart he always wanted to stay in contact. He may have been manipulated on an unconscious level to become estranged only to one parent by the other parent (most often the mother)."

When a child becomes an adult, he may want to pursue a relationship with family members he was forced to break communication with as a child, but it is very difficult to do it unless it is in secret. The child may feel he is doing something wrong or betraying his primary caregiver when he goes to visit the estranged family member. Many times, the relationship has been kept in secret, so it does not upset others.

Control

Many parents have a hard time respecting their adult child and his or her spouse as another family unit. Instead, they see them as simply an extension of their own family. There was never a gradual transition of letting go when the adult child left home. The parent still feels the need to hold on and control the adult child for whatever reason.

It is helpful to think of your adult child like a friend. Most people would not tell their friends what to do or demand something from them. The same should be said for your adult children. They are your friends now, not people to be scolded, controlled, or manipulated.

Of course, it is still good for adult children to listen to their parents and hear them out when they have something to say. They are older and wiser. Maybe not in every area, but they have lived longer and have seen a few things. Thoughtfully consider the parent's requests and try to be considerate of them, especially as they age. Proverbs 23:22 says this: "Listen to your father who gave you life, and do not despise your mother when she is old."

In the end, the Bible states that once a person is married, he or she becomes one flesh with the spouse (Mark 10:8-10). The marriage comes first. It is not healthy when the parents get into the middle of a marriage and their demands take priority over the spouse. This is not God's perfect design. When adult children leave home, they are no longer under orders from God to "obey." They are now commanded to "honor" (Ephesians 6:2).

Honor and respect do not go just one way. Healthy relationships are marked by a mutual respect for one another. Both parties recognize that the other has preferences and needs, depending on the stage of life. It is wise for the parent to learn to be a friend. Love, encourage, and accept the adult child and his or her spouse as another family. Work to understand each other's needs. Try to listen more than you speak. Smile and say "great" when your independent, adult child relays information to you. Don't give advice unless asked. Even then, tread carefully!

People-Pleasing

As Christians, I think it is hard to tell the difference between being a good Christian and people-pleasing. As I said earlier, this one thing almost destroyed me. I was the worst at setting boundaries. I said "yes" to everything that was asked of me, even at the cost of my husband, kids, and health. And then I was angry for saying "yes." I have since learned what people-pleasing is and how not to fall in that trap again, as it is unhealthy behavior. Over the years, I have come to understand that the root of people-pleasing is often the fear of rejection or the fear of failure.

I was afraid to say "no," because I feared any consequences of that answer. I wasn't secure enough about who I was outside of my family to draw boundaries, even if they were angry. I said "yes" to doing things because I wanted to be loved. Because I wanted to be the hero who could always save the day. I needed the constant approval. As a high achiever, I feared failure and the disappointment of others.

Eventually, this model fell apart. I couldn't do anything for anyone, not even myself. I was so sick and angry for being pulled in too many directions. I resented it whenever I said "yes" to something I did not want to do. I was mad at myself for not having the courage to say "no." I felt like a complete failure. I began to realize I could only do so much. My own family had to be my first priority. Now I think hard before I say "yes" to things that others ask of me. I make sure I want to do them. Then I am not angry, because I am choosing to do whatever it is out of love.

Sexual Choices

In doing my research on family estrangement, I discovered many stories of families who split because the adult child chose a life of sexual immorality. In all of my reading, I never found one case where estrangement actually helped bring the adult child to a place of repentance. But I sure read a lot of stories where abandonment and estrangement of a loved one destroyed the whole family. I only know to ask the question, "What would Jesus do?" My answer is love. Tough love is included. You can hate the sin and still love the sinner. You may have to set firm boundaries, but I think it is better than estrangement.

Your Family Rift or Estrangement

I encourage you to pray about the real reasons you have a family rift or total estrangement. Ask God to show you if you are doing anything that is destructive. You may be blinded to your own behavior. Let God show you the root of your family's problems. Dealing with your part of the problem could open up the relationship in ways you never thought possible. Be willing to be broken. Remove the pride from your life so you can see the truth.

Save your comments and tell God your expectations or hurts. He is listening to you. He alone knows your needs and the needs of your family. Your job is to work on yourself and leave the rest to Him. That is all you can change—you. If you are stuck and don't know the problem, I would prayerfully consider talking to someone who knows you and your family. Ask the hard questions. If you are willing to listen, your friend may be able to point out some of the issues. Friends know you well enough to see things you can't see. Sometimes even more than a counselor.

It is so much easier to see other people's problems than it is to see your own. Unfortunately, most of us don't want to ask our family friends or other family members, because we don't really want to hear the answer. The answer is hard to hear, and it is sometimes embarrassing. Once you hear the truth, it becomes reality. And that means you have to make a conscious choice to deal with the problem. I wish my family would have done this. I believe we would have dealt with our issues sooner. It would have saved us a whole lot of grief.

Introspection

1. Are any of these issues playing a part in your family rift or estrangement?
2. If you don't know, will you ask another family member or family friend for any insight as to why this has happened?
3. Will you address your part of the problem directly? Even if it is an addiction?
4. Will you swallow your pride, make amends, and change?
5. Are you willing to release your loved one to God and no longer control the outcome?
6. Will you start practicing real love?

Verses for Spiritual Warfare

Proverbs 12:15
　The way of fools seems right to them, but the wise listen to advice.

John 16:13
　But when he, the Spirit of truth, comes, he will guide you into all the truth. He will not speak on his own; he will speak only what he hears, and he will tell you what is yet to come.

Proverbs 25:28
　Like a city whose walls are broken through is a person who lacks self-control.

Proverbs 28:26
　Those who trust in themselves are fools, but those who walk in wisdom are kept safe.

Psalm 19:12-13
　But who can discern their own errors? Forgive my hidden faults. Keep your servant also from willful sins; may they not rule over me. Then I will be blameless, innocent of great transgression.

CHAPTER 7

I Choose to Forgive

Forgiveness is the most difficult subject for me to write about, because it is the thorn in my flesh. My Achilles heel. I feel I am the least qualified person to write this chapter, but I know it is something that needs to be addressed, and it is part of my story. You can blame a family split on any number of things—addiction, control, child abuse, lack of respect, money, mental illness, people-pleasing—but in the end, a lack of forgiveness is often the nail in the coffin. It almost destroyed me. It almost destroyed my whole family. I went down that path, rolled in the dirt, and got the T-shirt.

It is easy to dwell on everything that has happened and fantasize about what it would be like for the other party to get punished. Or just to dwell on what has happened and wallow in self-pity. When you continue to replay the events over and over in your head, you become even more traumatized. The "play" button is stuck day and night. You have the initial offense and then the amplified version going on in your head over and over again for years. (If this is happening to you, I would suggest a counselor to help you get unstuck.)

In the case of an actual crime, such as a sexual or physical offense, justice can be served through a court of law. But it will never be enough, no matter what the punishment. Even the death penalty won't cure the pain. At the end of the day, not forgiving the offender will only destroy you, no matter what has happened or how heinous the offense. Even if the offender is dead, you can continue to wallow in pain, soothing yourself. It is like you are stroking a wounded child and feeding him candy. One day, the candy is probably going to make the wounded child physically, mentally, or emotionally sick. You can't continue to feed the wounded child and not expect a bad outcome. Unforgiveness will materialize at some point.

Revenge

When we are bitter and can't let go, we deceive ourselves into thinking revenge will help us feel better and clear the slate. But the slate is never clear, no matter what you do. We think revenge will even it out. Instead, it escalates the problem to a new level (see chapter four). Paybacks never work.

Maybe you are afraid to let go of the feelings and let God administer justice in His time. Instead, you keep the offenses alive, so you can ensure "justice" will be done. I can tell you this much—that is a lie. Plotting revenge or asking God to pay back the offender is misguided, and it does not lead to true justice.

Instead, ask God to help you forgive. Pray for the offender. It is important to realize the offender can never truly give back what was taken from you. It is gone forever. It is better to release that loss to God and let Him heal the pain. Many people think that if they forgive, then it excuses what has been done. That is not true at all. It is releasing the offenses to God and letting Him be judge and jury. Nothing gets by Him. He knows, and He will deal with it in His time and in His way. When you step in and act as God, you do more harm to yourself than good.

We expect God to forgive us for our sins against Him, but He, in turn, asks us to forgive each other in the same way. Matthew 6:14-15 states the following: "For if you forgive other people when they sin against you, your Heavenly Father will also forgive you. But if you do not forgive others their sins, your Father will not forgive your sins." I would also refer you to the story of the wicked servant in Matthew 18. He was forgiven a large debt by his master but was unwilling to forgive the much smaller debt of a fellow servant. When the master heard of his actions, the wicked servant was put in jail. In the same way, God expects us to forgive the smaller debts since He has already forgiven us for such a large debt—our sin.

When we don't forgive, we put ourselves in jail. We are imprisoned by our own unforgiveness and are no longer free. Ironically, we are the only ones who have the key to get ourselves out. We have to decide to unlock the door and walk away from the anger and bitterness. No one else can do it for us. It took a long time for me to realize this concept. I had to suffer greatly before I came to this conclusion. What I have learned about unforgiveness is it will drag you to places you never wished to go. And it will cost a much higher price than you ever thought you would pay. It is a trap. Run from it, fast. Mentally choose to forgive when it comes up in your thought-life.

Forgiveness Is a Choice

Forgiveness is a choice. It is a choice you choose every day and every time you start to dwell on the pain. You have to decide you are going to make your brain stop thinking about it and move on to something else. It is hard. It takes discipline. Every time I start to wallow in my self-pity, I visualize myself drinking poison. I can trigger a Crohn's flare-up quickly if I don't get a hold of myself. It's just not worth it. I find the best distraction is worship music. It gets my mind on God and off of me.

I am still learning how to forgive easily and set boundaries all at once. This is a very delicate balance, since I tend toward the extremes of either people-pleasing or remaining bitter. I feel like a toddler waddling around on two feet, barely making progress. I keep coming back to 1 Corinthians 13, the love chapter. Verses 4-5 says, "Love is patient, love is kind. It does not envy, it does not boast, it is not proud. It does not dishonor others, it is not self-seeking, it is not easily angered, it keeps no record of wrongs."

It doesn't mean we pretend we are not hurt, cover it up, or stay in denial. Real forgiveness means we are fully aware of what happened—every painful detail—and we still choose to let it go. We can't humanly forget the offenses, but we can choose not to remember. This is real forgiveness, just like God does for us. He chooses not to remember our sin, even though He knows every painful detail of what we have done. This doesn't mean we go back to abusive behavior. It just means we have released it to God to deal with it as He sees fit.

What About Abuse?

Love doesn't mean staying in a relationship if the other party is abusive. The family member may not be trustworthy. You may have to love from afar. The Bible says in Romans 12:18, "If it is possible, as far as it depends on you, live at peace with everyone." This means to get your side of the problem straight. Make amends where necessary and try to live in peace—if possible. It may not be possible. No one wants to be trashed by a family member or put in harm's way physically, mentally, spiritually, or emotionally.

Total forgiveness means not being angry even if there is no reconciliation. The outcome is up to God. Whatever happens, you will not manipulate the situation or seek retribution for your pain. This is hard for many parents who want to push their way back into an adult child's life. The relationship may be so damaged that the adult child will never feel safe again. If the adult child isn't interested, then there is no use trying. Both parties need to be willing to work things out.

Dr. Deborah Newman, who is a licensed counselor, assures me that forgiveness, communication, and healthy boundaries can allow even a victim of abuse to experience healthy interactions with family members. The key is to be honest—sometimes brutally honest. It would take a lot of change and repentance before that could happen, but it is possible. And the same goes for a parent who has experienced horrible behavior from an adult child. The key is repentance, forgiveness, and true change.

You have to really listen to the Holy Spirit on how to proceed once you do start forgiving. It took seven years for my family to come to a place of forgiveness. And we are still forgiving. It isn't a "one and done" thing. Issues still come up, and we have to work through them. There is no way to bypass this if you want real healing.

Forgiving Myself and God

I had to not only work on forgiving others, but I also had to work on forgiving myself and forgiving God. I was angry with myself because I didn't know how to make my family functional. A part of me had to let go of that perfect child in that perfect family everyone thought we had. I wanted to please everyone. And I wanted to change everyone to fit that perfect family. That was the wrong mindset. We are not a perfect family. We are a forgiven family. And I can only control my behavior—no one else's behavior.

As for God, this one was a little more difficult. I was angry He allowed my estrangement to happen in the first place. We are all Christians and know better. He could have stopped it, yet He didn't. How does a loving God allow bad things to happen to good people? We all face this question at one time or another. And my answer is going to be incomplete. First of all, none of us are good. Second, it requires a leap of faith to believe God is good, and He loves us even when bad things happen. Real love means giving us a free will to choose. We are not puppets. He will not control or manipulate us into behaving as we should. We choose everyday how we are going to live our lives. When we don't follow biblical principles, there will be consequences.

I have come to believe my situation will bring God glory in the end, if I let Him. God is good, and everything goes through His loving hands first. The Bible says in Romans 8:28, "And we know that in all things God works for the good of those who love him, who have been called according to his purpose." I trust Him with the good and the bad so that He may be glorified even in the messes. I can't see everything now, but I will see clearly someday. I can't tell you how hard it is for me to say those words, because the byproduct of the pain in my childhood has been distrust. Trusting God has not come easy for me. I question God and sometimes don't like His answers. But eventually, I lay down my hands and rest in His lap. For me, rest has meant reconciliation.

Working Toward Reconciliation

For me and my family, reconciliation has required a delicate balance. We have tried to meet somewhere in the middle. The balance for your family will look different from my family. It may even look different for each relationship. If you care enough about the relationship, find your middle. I can't tell you how to work it out, but I can tell you that you will need a lot of forgiveness to hear the other side and meet in the middle.

For the last couple of years, we have slowly gone back and talked through some painful situations. Only a little at a time. It is all we can take. Small doses. We try to own our respective parts and then release them. This has been the best way for us to move forward. We are all committed to forgiving as we move along. And then try to make changes where we went wrong.

My suggestion is for you not to accuse others but speak the truth lovingly and do a lot of listening. You have to leave your pride at the door and be willing to see the truth in its entirety. Once you have worked through things, it will take time to build trust. Communication and positive feedback are helpful in avoiding missteps as you continue to move forward. It is not easy to forgive and start over, but it is so much better than being estranged. You can choose to either be hardened by life's losses, or you can allow God to use the most difficult valleys to conform you to the image of Christ. I choose to forgive and be conformed to Christ.

I believe forgiveness is the one thing that sets us apart from the world. It is what makes Christians different. Think of all the amazing stories about how victims have come back and looked their offender in the eyes and said, "I forgive." Not, "It is okay." Just the simple words, "I forgive you." In turn, many of those offenders have come to Christ because of this amazing gift. They are drawn to a love that cannot be rationalized in human terms. God's love can only be explained as supernatural. As I have stated before, it doesn't mean you have to return to a toxic situation when you do this. Forgiveness and reconciliation are two different things.

I want you to know that I understand that estrangement might need to be a lifelong reality. However, forgiveness is mandatory for your own health. I hope you will read the rest of this book and follow the suggestions in chapter 11, even if you never find a way to have a family connection. At least you can know that you have done everything that God asks of you.

Your Family

I don't know what happened in your family, and maybe you don't really know either. My guess is that if you are reading this book, it is serious. I found that looking back at my family history helped me to forgive. Learning what happened to my parents gave me context on how they developed their parenting style. Most parents try to do the best they can. Many times, they are drawing from a well that is empty. Maybe your parents didn't have it to give to you. Whatever "it" is.

You have to consider the things that happened in their families of origin. They may have their own set of issues. They probably need to forgive some things too. This is not an excuse but a starting point. It is hard to fully comprehend why your family relationship is strained if you don't know what happened to your parents. If you are able to dig up some history, it is sometimes easier to work through it and forgive.

A personal example: One side of my family is Italian. Digging a little has helped me to realize how that side of the family did things. I don't exactly agree with it all, but it does help me understand. This, in turn, helped me to forgive. We are commanded to forgive no matter your origin or your traumas. It all comes down to a choice. Choosing to forgive is the best way to get free. For me, forgiveness led to reconciliation. In the next chapter I will share with you how it all happened. It was truly miraculous.

Introspection

1. Is what you are doing working?
2. If not, will you try forgiveness?
3. Will you choose to forgive every time you start to harbor resentment?
4. Will you start praying for the ones who have hurt you?
5. Will you ask God to bless whoever has hurt you?

Verses for Spiritual Warfare

Colossians 3:13
  Bear with each other and forgive one another if any of you has a grievance against someone. Forgive as the Lord forgave you.

Mark 11:25
  And when you stand praying, if you hold anything against anyone, forgive them, so that your Father in heaven may forgive you your sins.

Matthew 6:15
  But if you do not forgive others their sins, your Father will not forgive your sins.

Ephesian 4:32
  Be kind and compassionate to one another, forgiving each other, just as in Christ God forgave you.

Matthew 18:21-22
  Then Peter came to Jesus and asked, "Lord, how many times shall I forgive my brother or sister who sins against me? Up to seven times?" Jesus answered, "I tell you, not seven times, but seventy-times seven."

CHAPTER 8

Reconciliation: Eight Miracles

As I said earlier, my counselor told me that, considering the age of my parents and the length of time apart, there was about a 99% chance we would never work it out. He told me to prepare myself for when they passed away, because the grief was going to be totally different from a regular family death. I would be dealing with abandonment, the lack of closure, and lost hope. He left me with these words: "But God ... But God can work a miracle. It is not healthy to bank on such little hope, but you can pray for a miracle." And so I did. And a miracle is what I got. Not just one miracle, but eight miracles.

A New Beginning

The miracles didn't come overnight. It was a series of miracles over exactly a one-year time period. Bookends from one year to the next. It also didn't happen the way I thought it might. I had to learn to be flexible. We all did. When you pray for your family to reconcile, you must be willing to let God work in the way He sees fit. You may not like the way He chooses to work, but do not be stiff-necked. God hates stubbornness.

The Fast

In December of 2016, I felt God was leading me to fast for my family. There is nothing worse than being estranged from your family during the holidays. As I discussed before, it is painful on so many levels. I was grieved because October of 2016 had marked seven years of no communication with my parents. I was already dreading future holiday seasons of explaining, sadness, justification, and emptiness. I missed seeing my middle sister, parents, cousins, aunts, nieces, and nephews. I was tired of hearing family news through Facebook or second-hand through friends or other family members. I was tired of the emotions of another year and no resolution.

At the end of the 2016 holidays, I asked God to let it be the last Christmas I would spend away from my family. I wanted a change. I prayed for Him to show me what to do so Christmas of 2017 would be different. I no longer wanted to do the holidays with half of my family. I wanted all of my family. Both sides. It was then God prompted me to fast.

I tried to talk myself out of it. How was depriving myself of food and praying for a certain amount of time going to change anything? I had already been praying off and on for the last seven years, and nothing had changed. God lovingly reminded me through Scripture how certain situations take deep intercession to see any real movement (Isaiah 58:6). I decided to be obedient and do it. God had prompted me to fast before, but I never could give up food for that long.

There was never a real determination to pray about the things that needed to change, so I never fasted before then. But this time, it was different. I was willing to go 48 hours without food because I was so completely frustrated by the lack of progress over the years. I chose the first Tuesday and Wednesday of the first week in January 2017. It was a good way to start the New Year. No parties to tempt me to eat, since the holidays were over. During my fast, I decided to pray for each family member intensely. Most of all, I prayed for my father.

I specifically prayed God would talk to him in his dreams. I asked God to show him it was time to reconcile. Since nothing was happening while he was awake, I thought maybe God would talk to him while he was sleeping. God could talk to him in a way that was less threatening. I don't know where I got that. I just thought it would be a good way into his heart.

The First Miracle

This is when the first miracle occurred. God told my middle sister (the one not estranged from our parents) to fast at the same time, during the first week in January. We were barely talking, so she had no idea I was fasting too. It was a terrible time for her to do it, but she did it anyway. Her health was suffering. It was a big sacrifice.

The Second Miracle

My dad had a dream on Wednesday (the second day my sister and I were both fasting). God showed him in a dream that I was coming home. He saw me eating dinner in his dining room with my mom and him. My father woke up in the middle of the night and shook my mom. He told her he had a dream that I was coming back to the family. He then proceeded to tell her his dream. My mom was a little skeptical and said, "Ok, go back to bed." It was at this point my dad knew something had changed. Truthfully, I prayed for a fire and brimstone type dream, but I guess I can't complain about the outcome—God did talk to my father in a dream. Be flexible!

The Third Miracle

The Friday of the same week I fasted, my dad called my husband. He wanted to meet with him privately to discuss the situation. My sister and I had fasted Tuesday and Wednesday, and my dad called Friday. I think that is pretty miraculous after seven years of no talking. My husband decided to go see my parents that Friday evening. He didn't tell me in case it went bad.

It took my husband 24 hours to process the evening. The conversation wasn't filled with a bunch of apologies; it was more of a talk about making peace. I had envisioned there would be apologies if we ever talked again. That didn't happen. My husband wasn't sure how I was going to handle the whole situation since I was expecting one thing and got another.

My middle sister called me that Saturday morning. She spent an hour talking with me. She became my entry point back into the family. It was her mediation that helped things move along. You don't want the mediator stuck in the middle for very long, but it is good to have someone inside the family helping you navigate back into the family.

After I got off the phone with her, my husband told me he had been to my parents' house the night before. I was overjoyed at first. I couldn't believe how God worked so quickly after I prayed and fasted. Then anger set in. I was mad it took seven years for my dad to call. And I was expecting an apology. It took me two weeks to think and pray through the anger. I had gotten what I prayed for, but I wasn't happy about some of the packaging.

The Fourth Miracle

The third week in January, I was at my Bible Study Fellowship gathering. Our leader was talking about forgiveness and letting God work in His own way. She talked for 45 minutes about it. By the end of the lesson, I wanted to stand up and yell, "Ok, I got it. I have had enough. I can't take any more. I'll call them!" I was so convicted; it was like there was a fire under my chair where I was sitting. I was squirming around the whole time, completely uncomfortable with the words my teaching leader was saying. I was also in shock. I had never heard a lesson like this before—EVER.

It felt like there was no one else in the room but me. God had given me a CLEAR sign that it was time to move ahead. I was so bound up by fear that I was paralyzed. Apparently, I needed my Bible Study Fellowship teaching leader to nudge me along. I called my parents the next day, and we talked. There were no real apologies made. Just a time to talk and catch up. It was a sign of peace. My mom then asked my husband and me to come to dinner. By the time we finally came, it was February 2017. We agreed to meet them at their house. We drove down to where they lived and had dinner together.

The Fifth Miracle

At the dinner table that night, my dad told me about the dream he had. He told me he dreamed we were eating dinner together at their table … as we were eating dinner together… at their table.

Let's just review this in case you didn't catch everything.

1. My sister, unbeknownst to me until months later, had been fasting at the exact same time I was fasting (the first week in January).
2. God spoke to my father in a dream the second day of fasting, just as I had prayed.
3. It had been seven years with no talking, and my dad called two days after my sister and I fasted.
4. God designed the lesson in Bible Study Fellowship that following week to talk to me directly about forgiveness. And to prompt me to move forward.
5. We were eating dinner together at the dining room table, just as my father dreamed we would.

You can call that coincidence. I don't think so. This was God. It was one miracle after another. As they say in the commercials … but wait, there is more!

The Sixth Miracle

The next miracle may seem a bit odd. While I was estranged from my parents, I kept having this recurring dream that I was in the hospital holding my dad's hand. I always thought it was a peculiar dream. I thought it was my mind preparing me for the fact that I would say goodbye to my dad on his deathbed. Or that it was because

I saw him in the hospital when he had a heart attack. I couldn't figure it out.

That was not it at all. This is how the dream came to be fulfilled. It had been around six months since my parents and I had started talking again. Our relationship had been improving at a slow, steady pace. I had been trying to go see them about once a month. They live 45 minutes away, so it wasn't like I could just drop in. We had to plan our visits.

This particular day I was coming to see my parents, my dad was sick. My mom said to come anyway. My dad would just be in bed, but my mom and I would still spend a bit of time together. I arrived in the early afternoon. My dad was lying on the couch, and he didn't look good. My father had been in the emergency room the night before. They sent him home. The doctor thought it might be the flu. The hospital wasn't sure what he had, but they didn't see the need to keep him overnight.

An hour or two after I arrived at the house, we noticed he was progressively getting worse. My mom and I decided he needed to go back to the hospital. After a few hours, the doctors decided it was really serious, and he needed to go to a larger hospital in Dallas. My mom had been up the night before taking care of my father. She was exhausted. She was not physically up to the drive to Dallas. She went home instead.

They sent my dad on by ambulance. I decided to follow the ambulance up to Dallas and stay with him through the night until he was diagnosed, stabilized, and checked into a room. He was really sick. It was the strangest thing. I remember holding his hand through the evening thinking, "Six months ago we weren't even talking, and now I'm in complete control of his care. This is weird. What are the chances of this happening?"

Then I suddenly remembered my recurring dream. I had been holding my dad's hand while he was in a hospital bed. All those times I was dreaming the hospital dream, God was saying my relationship would be restored to the point where I would even be the one solely in charge of his care for a night.

Amazingly, when I was checking my father into the hospital that night, he was asked who was to make decisions for him. My father pointed to me and in a clear voice said my name and my mother's name. He chose me after all we had been through. You could tell he knew what he was saying. I almost started crying right there. Six months ago, I had not talked to him in seven years. And in that moment, I was making health decisions for my father. The whole thing was surreal.

There had never been any apologies up to that point, but I knew something happened that night between us. Something in my heart changed. Interestingly enough, I have never had that dream again. After it was fulfilled, it went away.

The Seventh Miracle

I had prayed a year earlier, November of 2016, that it would be the last Christmas away from my family. I asked

God to restore my family, so I could be with them for Christmas of 2017. It almost didn't happen. My parents invited our family and some extended family to join them on Christmas Day. I hadn't seen some of these family members since I was a child because of the first estrangement from my grandparents. While I had been away, my parents had reconciled with them. What a miracle that God had been working on the relationships with my extended family too.

Two days before Christmas, my mom started getting sick. By Christmas Eve, she was down on the couch. She went to the emergency room, and they said she had pneumonia. They gave her medication and sent her home to rest. They told her not to do anything. The doctors wanted her to stay in bed. My mom was so upset. She didn't want to cancel Christmas. We had all been praying for our family to be together for a long time. It had not happened for years. Somehow God gave my mom the power to push through even though she was sick.

We all came together on Christmas Day. It was a wonderful time. During the present exchange, my family even gave me the family gag gift. I was back home. We laughed and just enjoyed being together. It took 30 years for that moment to happen. The prayer I prayed a year earlier was answered. I had asked God to let Christmas 2016 be the last holiday without my extended family. I had no idea God would go above and beyond and bring back my dad's side of the family too. (They were part of the first estrangement.) It was a Christmas miracle indeed.

The Eighth Miracle

Fast forward a couple of weeks to the first Tuesday in January of 2018. I was sitting in Bible Study Fellowship. (If you recall, I fasted exactly one year earlier, January 2017, and asked God to talk to my father.) On this particular day, my BSF leader was sick, so our class joined another class. We were going through the discussion questions, and the conversation moved to prayer. Someone asked about God speaking to people in their dreams. She wanted to know if it was biblical to pray for this to happen.

One of the ladies said, "Yes, it's in the Bible. I think you can pray for God to speak to people in their dreams." Then she mentioned a few scriptures. One is Job 33:14-16 which says, "For God speaks again and again, though people do not recognize it. He speaks in dreams, in visions of the night, when deep sleep falls on people as they lie in their beds. He whispers in their ears and terrifies them with warnings" (NLT). I was about to fall out of my chair because I knew this was the one-year anniversary of my fasting. A year ago exactly, I had prayed for God to speak to my dad in a dream. I spoke up to my class and said, "Yes, it is possible. It does happen, because I did it a year ago today." Then I told the class the whole story.

Everyone was a little dumbfounded. I wasn't even supposed to be in this class, and here we were, having this conversation about praying for God to speak in dreams EXACTLY a year later to the day. And I was able to give God the glory for the whole thing.

A few people came up to me afterward and talked to me about it. They had people from whom they were estranged too. Hearing from me definitely strengthened their faith and gave them hope. It was then I knew I needed to write a book, so more people would hear my story. I knew that the principles I applied had worked. I wanted to tell other people how they could find hope if their families had fallen apart. I wanted them to know it is possible to come home, even after a long estrangement.

God moved in my family because we were all obedient. My middle sister and I prayed and fasted, my dad called, and then my mom followed up with a second phone call. If we all had not acted when God moved us forward, this book would probably not be in existence. I could have hardened my heart and not believed God was actually answering my prayers when my father called my husband that very first time. I had it all in my head on how our reconciliation should be played out, but my scenario didn't allow for the Holy Spirit to move in a miraculous way. When God is in something, you will know it. You must act on your faith even when you are fearful and can't see the path ahead. Otherwise, you will stay stuck in the past forever.

Introspection

1. Will you fervently pray and ask God to restore your family?
2. Will you ask God to change your heart if it has hardened against certain family members?
3. Will you obey whatever the answer?
4. Will you be willing to allow God to work out the reconciliation in His way and His time?
5. Will you stand firm on who you are in Christ, no matter what happens with your family?

Verses for Spiritual Warfare

Isaiah 61:1, 3-4, 7

The Spirit of the Sovereign Lord is on me, because the Lord has anointed me to proclaim good news to the poor. He has sent me to bind up the brokenhearted, to proclaim freedom for the captives and release from darkness the prisoners.

And provide for those who grieve in Zion—to bestow on them a crown of beauty instead of ashes, the oil of joy instead of mourning, and a garment of praise instead of a spirit of despair. They will be called oaks of righteousness, a planting of the Lord for the display of his splendor. They will rebuild the ancient ruins and restore the places long devastated; they will renew the ruined cities that have been devastated for generations.

Instead of your shame you will receive a double portion, and instead of disgrace you will rejoice in your inheritance. And so you will inherit a double portion in your land, and everlasting joy will be yours.

Isaiah 43:5-6

Do not be afraid, for I am with you; I will bring your children from the east and gather you from the west. I will say to the north, 'Give them up!' and to the south, 'Do not hold them back.' Bring my sons from afar and my daughters from the ends of the earth—

CHAPTER 9
Coming Home to Family

Coming home is joyous. Unfortunately, after everyone has readjusted, the same problems can reappear. It is Satan's best attempt to keep you from reintegrating. If I told you it was easy coming back into my family, I would be lying. My family of origin grieved losing us. But they moved on. After seven years, they created a new life. They started a new normal. We all created new habits and traditions for holidays, birthdays, etc.

I found different friends to be with at the holidays and even other families who stepped in for me when my parents weren't around. You try to do the best you can and make a life. When I came back, I had a lot of thoughts in my head:

- You don't belong here anymore.
- You don't fit in.

- Everyone is angry with you for leaving.
- No one trusts you.
- No one understands why you left.
- This isn't going to work.
- Your parents don't love you.
- You are a bad child.
- No one knows what to say to you.
- People are staring at you.
- This is awkward
- No one has changed
- No one is going to respect my boundaries
- You can't do this again
- You don't have the emotional energy

I could go on, but I think you get the point. Let's face it. It is awkward, and you may even feel some shame. Many times, there is a lot of fear. There are going to be blips in conversation that refer to a time when you weren't there. It is hard to just smile and not cringe. But that is what you have to do. Admit it is awkward and keep slowly moving forward. Face your fears head on and combat the shame.

This time of reintegration is very tender because everyone is testing the waters. Many times the same issues come back to surface, and no one knows how to deal with them differently. The adult child or parent gets angry again, and then everyone gives up because nothing has truly changed. Everyone is still acting in the exact same family roles as before. Here is an example of what I mean. This story reflects the situation of so many people who have tried to return but, in the end, leave for good.

Stacy's Story

Not too long ago, I talked with a woman named "Stacy" who had been estranged from her parents for many years. The reason she left her family was because she was physically and emotionally worn down from dealing with her parent's constant demands (control). After an enormous amount of pressure from other Christians, Stacy decided to go back to her family of origin because her parents had assured her they would change. Stacy also felt it was the right thing to do since she was a Christian. Unfortunately, the reconciliation didn't stick.

When Stacy started to tell the reason why she left a second time, she started to cry. I could barely understand what she was saying at that point. My heart broke watching her try to explain every painful detail. You could see her mind replaying the scene like it happened yesterday when, in fact, it had occurred many years ago. After Stacy calmed down, she told me that not too long after the reconciliation, she decided to visit her parent's church. On that particular evening, the church had provided a meal beforehand. When Stacy went to sit down at the table to eat dinner with her kids, a woman at the other end of the table said, "Oh, I know you. You're the problem child." And then she looked at Stacy in disgust. Stacy was horrified. And she was embarrassed.

It was at that moment Stacy realized her mother had been speaking badly about her within the church community while she was estranged. Her mother's unforgiveness had spilled over and colored people's opinion of her. This incident caused an enormous amount of shame for Stacy. After experiencing this and a few other hurtful things, Stacy gave up and left her family of origin for good because she knew real changes had not been made.

I have seen this situation more times than I would like to admit. Parents and children cycling in and out of the family because the root problems were never truly resolved, and the retaliation tactics were so far reaching there was no turning back. The water had been poisoned, and the damage was done.

I believe Satan wants to take any opportunity he can to destroy your family's reconciliation. Remember who the adversary is here. It is not your family. It is Satan. Just because you have reconciled doesn't mean Satan won't try to push you back out again. When those painful thoughts come into your head, and they will, you have to combat them with the truth. You need to take your rightful place in your family of origin, if at all possible. It was given to you at birth. Your place in the family is important. Don't let anyone, including yourself, keep you from making the last step into the reconciliation process.

You Are Loved

I have gone back to one verse over and over again throughout the whole process of my family estrangement. It is my favorite verse, because I know that I am loved, and God put me on this earth for a purpose. He gave me my family. I will not let Satan take them away from me.

It is Psalm 139:13-18:

> For you created my inmost being; you knit me together in my mother's womb, I praise you because I am fearfully and wonderfully made; your works are wonderful, I know that full well. My frame was not hidden from you when I was made in the secret place, when I was woven together in the depths of the earth. Your eyes saw my unformed body; all the days ordained for me were written in your book before one of them came to be. How precious to me are your thoughts, God! How vast is the sum of them! Were I to count them, they would outnumber the grains of sand—when I awake, I am still with you.

God uniquely placed you in your mother's womb. He meant for you to be in your family. It is Satan who wants you to be ripped away. Start fasting and praying, my precious friend. If you do go back, be prepared to start back where you left off. There is a honeymoon phase, but then as you settle in, life presents itself with the same problems. Situations arise, and those old issues will rear their ugly head. Some people think once you reconcile, all the issues magically disappear. They don't. This is your chance to do things differently. If you are considering going back to your family of origin, make sure you practice your new behaviors, so the family doesn't split again. Here are few suggestions you and your family can follow when interacting with each other:

- Admit when wrong
- Make amends
- Give advice only when asked
- Be respectful, kind, and supportive
- Be flexible
- Share power equally
- Forgive easily

It is hard to break family patterns, especially if you have been doing things the same way for most of your life. That is why it is important to be working on yourself before you go back, so you don't repeat the same patterns. Your changes will make others have to adjust to you. Going home is a slow process of reintegration. Don't rush it. I am grateful God worked in my family while I was gone, and I had the benefit of coming back to changed hearts. Otherwise, I am not sure I would have been able to return due to my health.

There are many of you who will not be going home, at least any time soon, because it is not safe. Or your adult child is not coming home to you. You have prayed, cried, and begged God, but nothing has happened so far. Preparing to come home is not the only situation in which God would have you pray fervently and seek to be conformed to Christ's image. In the next chapter, I will share some of what I learned about God's work in the silence.

Introspection

1. Are you fearful about going back into your family?
2. Will you continue to let God renew your thinking about your place in the family?
3. Will you put those shameful thoughts away and no longer listen to them when they come to mind?
4. Are you making a way for your family member to return safely?
5. Have you made the necessary changes in your life so your loved one will stay?

Verses for Spiritual Warfare

1 Peter 1:22
> Now that you have purified yourselves by obeying the truth so that you have sincere love for each other, love one another deeply, from the heart.

1 Corinthians 13:4-5
> Love is patient, love is kind. It does not envy, it does not boast, it is not proud. It does not dishonor others, it is not self-seeking, it is not easily angered, it keeps no record of wrongs.

Psalm 40:1-3
> I waited patiently for the Lord; he turned to me and heard my cry. He lifted me out of the slimy pit, out of the mud and mire; he set my feet on a rock and gave me a firm place to stand. He put a new song in my mouth, a hymn of praise to our God. Many will see and fear the lord and put their trust in Him.

Zephaniah 3:17
> The Lord your God is with you, the Mighty Warrior who saves. He will take great delight in you; in his love he will no longer rebuke you but will rejoice over you with singing.[2]

---

[2] How remarkable is that? God is singing over you!

CHAPTER 10
When God is Silent

Silence. I don't like being quiet. It is awkward. I like talking, noise, and action. I think many of us feel more powerful when we are working toward a solution. Or fixing a problem. But what if there is no solution to be found in your family right now? You have pushed, pulled, talked, and made lots of noise to no avail. Now there is silence. There is nothing left to say.

You are forced to simply wait for something to change. It is just you and your thoughts. You may start running situations over in your head and reliving the words of the past. Wondering if it would have made a difference had you said something a certain way or done something different. But it is too late now. It is quiet.

There is almost nothing worse than waiting for God to move in a situation. You start questioning what you thought was right and second guessing who God is. This is where all the lies manifest themselves. You start believing God is not capable of untangling your family mess or that He doesn't really care about your situation. On the surface, it can look like nothing is happening. Let me assure you, something is happening. You just can't see it. If you are praying for God to work, then He is working. It may not be at the speed you like, but He is still moving.

Abraham and Sarah

Think about Abraham and Sarah. All those years waiting for the promised child. Nothing. Year after year went by in silence, and they started wondering if God had really told them Sarah would have a child. They got tired of waiting and let Hagar, Sarah's handmaiden, sleep with Abraham. Yow! She became pregnant and produced a male heir—Ishmael. Abraham and Sarah thought they were helping God out by pushing the promise through another way. They didn't wait or believe God could work on their behalf, because He was taking too long. He was silent.

It was 25 years after God promised they would have a child that Isaac was born. Abraham was 100 years old, and Sarah was 90 years old. That is a long time to wait! (I thought seven years was a long time to wait on my family.) Waiting is hard. Doubt creeps in, and then we are tempted to manipulate situations. It is important not to miss what God is saying and be obedient as to how HE wants to work.

Job

Abraham is not the only person in the Bible who experienced silence. After Job lost everything—property, livestock, servants, his children—God never explained why. Job never knew God had given Satan permission to test him to see if he would be a faithful servant of God, even without all his blessings. Job had to suffer through the circumstances and live with the quietness of God. In the last three chapters of Job, God finally answered. He spoke to him in a whirlwind and put Job in his place. God said, "Job, you challenge Almighty God; will you give up now, or will you answer?" Then God proceeded to ask Job 77 questions. Wow! I don't think I would want to have been in Job's place.

In Job 42:2-3, Job says, "I know that you can do all things: no purpose of yours can be thwarted. You asked, 'Who is this that obscures my plans without knowledge?' Surely I spoke of things I did not understand, things too wonderful for me to know."

It is important for us to come to the same conclusion. We have to trust God and stop wrestling with His sovereignty. His plan is good, even when it seems bad. In *Life on the Brick Pile,* Jim Denison writes, "God allows and sometimes causes suffering in our lives in order to bring us back to our first love—himself."[3]

---

3 Denison, James C. *Life on the Brick Pile: Answers to Suffering from the Letters of Revelation.* Mercer University Press, 1997, p. 49.

David

Another biblical example is David, who waited at least 15 years from the time of his anointing to become king of Israel. Saul chased him around in the desert trying to kill him for many of those years. David wrote many of the Psalms during that time, crying out to God and wondering where He was. But he still trusted Him despite his circumstances. The same goes for Moses. He spent 40 years waiting in Midian before God told him to lead His people out of Egypt. If there is one thing I have learned, it is that God is often "slow." He does things on His clock, not mine. God is not bound by time. He already sees and knows when He is going to answer our prayers.

Jesus

The most powerful example of God's silence in the biblical narrative occurred when Jesus was on the cross. Jesus said, "My God, my God, why have you forsaken me" (Matthew 27:46). God was silent. He let His own child suffer through pain and horrific rejection. He may have turned His head when it happened, but He did not leave. He knew what was happening. When Jesus was in the grave for three days, there was silence again. But big things were happening. No one could see it, but God was working the greatest miracle ever.

Sometimes what looks like the end to us is actually just a pause. God is rearranging things. He might even be resurrecting something into new life. Whatever the problem, God knows what is happening with your family. He knows that you have been waiting. I can't tell you how it will all end, but I can tell you that He wants to bring life out of dead situations. He wants dry bones to come alive. He can use your specific situation for good, in some way, if you let Him.

Silence in My Family

In chapter three, I shared the timeline of what happened in the seven years I was away from my family. For a few years, nothing at all happened. God was silent on the matter of my family. I was hearing from Him on other matters, but not on the one thing about which I was talking to Him the most. I struggled with His silence. I felt abandoned. And I was angry. I told God He wasn't capable of working in my family. I shook my fist at Him a few times and told Him that He wasn't big enough to change everyone's hearts.

I thought if I hurled a bunch of insults at Him, I would coax Him out of hiding. Force Him to do something to prove Himself. This reminds me of what the people were saying when Jesus was dying on the cross. They told Jesus to prove Himself and come down. But God had bigger plans. Jesus didn't need to prove Himself to the people. And God didn't need to prove Himself to me. All of my insults didn't work. God just kept being silent. He was not uncomfortable with His silence either. But I sure was. I was convinced He left me alone with nowhere to turn.

I wrestled with God like Jacob wrestled with God (actually the pre-incarnate Christ) in Genesis 32. I kept fighting with God, questioning His sovereignty. I couldn't understand why He would allow me to be estranged from my family. And why He didn't do something to stop it. Most of all, I couldn't understand why He was silent for years. Nothing. Nada. Zilch. I wanted action. Just like Jacob, after wrestling for a long period of time, my "hip" was displaced. During year six, I experienced my own family crisis with my child. It was that situation that broke me. After that, I was worn out. I stopped trying to fight God, and I started praying.

When things get hard, we equate God's silence with abandonment. Silence does not mean the absence of God. God is everywhere. He intimately knows you and your situation. But when He is silent, we often respond inappropriately. We start believing lies. Like Abraham and Sarah, we start questioning His goodness, His character, and His power. We lose hope, because we can neither see nor feel Him in the darkness. We can't always know God's reasons for being silent, but we can learn to respond rightly when He is.

Here are a few things to do when God is silent:

1. **Focus on Him.** Keep reminding yourself of God's character. There are many Bible studies that focus on God's names and what they mean. Or you can look them up and write them down. Keep reminding yourself of

who He is and what He has done. Tell yourself the truth. Don't believe the lies. When God is silent, Satan loves to assault you with his garbage. He wants you to doubt everything you know about God.

2. **Pursue God.** Pray, get into His word, and worship at a local church. God works mightily through His people in His church. All the things I recommend in chapter 11 will help if you go through a long period of silence. Many people run from God when nothing is happening. Realize this is a test of your faith. Run to Him, not away from Him.

3. **Surround yourself with the right friends who will encourage you.** Job had terrible friends when God was silent. They didn't help him at all. They spoke lies and didn't understand the situation. Find people who will love you and encourage you, even when your situation looks and sounds horrible on the surface. Who you spend your time with matters to your spiritual health.

4. **Trust God.** Believe that He is working on your behalf. God knows you better than you know yourself. You can trust Him with everything. God's timeline is very different from our own. In my family, we needed time for other situations to resolve before we were ready to deal with each other. There were things we needed to learn and hearts that needed to be softened. This took time. Some family situations need more time than others.

I realize there are situations that may never get resolved, like the situation with my grandparents. I had to release that to God and trust that it was the best thing for me and my family. There are times when it is clearly not safe to get back into a relationship. Whatever the problem, you can expect God to keep working.

Part of my family is still estranged from us. I have had to give this to God. I can't manipulate something that is out of my control. He has to work in His way and in His time, like He did in my life. He may choose to do something miraculous and use it for His glory, or He may remain silent on the matter and still use it for His glory.

When God is silent, it is hard. And it may go on for many years, like it did for me. When a breakthrough did come, though, it made me more grateful. I was ready for movement. Even if I didn't exactly like the way God was moving, it was better than nothing.

If God does see fit to move on your behalf, and you do begin a relationship with your family again, remember that it will be filled with challenges. In the meantime, there are a lot of things to do while you wait. The suggestions I included helped me. I believe they can help in your healing process too.

Introspection

1. Will you trust God in the silence?
2. Even when it looks dark and hopeless, will you continue to seek Him through prayer, worship, and reading His word?
3. Will you find a Bible-believing church and surround yourself with encouraging people who will intercede on your behalf?
4. Will you no longer wallow in self-pity?
5. Will you give up your anger and trade it for peace?

Verses for Spiritual Warfare

Psalm 38:15
Lord, I wait for you; you will answer, Lord my God.

Hebrews 11:1
Now faith is confidence in what we hope for and assurance about what we do not see.

Lamentations 3:25-26
The Lord is good to those whose hope is in him, to the one who seeks him; it is good to wait quietly for the salvation of the Lord.

Micah 7:7
But as for me, I watch in hope for the Lord, I wait for God my Savior; my God will hear me.

Isaiah 40:31
But those who hope in the Lord will renew their strength. They will soar on wings like eagles; they will run and not grow weary, they will walk and not be faint.

CHAPTER 11

How to Heal from the Pain

I wish I could give you a magic bullet or formula to help your situation. Unfortunately, it doesn't work that way. But as I've shared some in the previous chapters, there were some specific things I did that helped me heal and gave me hope when my family fell apart.

This chapter is a compilation of suggestions I have recommended throughout the book. I put them together for you so you would have an easy reference as it can take a long time to do all of them. I did these things at different times during the seven years I was gone. The first year, all I did was get healthy. And I prayed. Each year I focused on different aspects of my healing process. You can't do all of these at once. Choose where to start according to your situation. It doesn't matter if you are the parent or the adult child. It will work for either situation. Don't be overwhelmed. I do believe with my whole heart these suggestions can help you (like they helped me), because they are based on the truths of God's word.

Suggestions

1. **Find faith.** If you have not accepted Jesus as your Lord and Savior, it will be difficult to get traction in some of these other areas.[4] Especially in the area of forgiveness. These steps can only be accomplished with supernatural power. If you don't know Jesus Christ, then it is time to reconsider your faith. Without His Holy Spirit working within you, none of these suggestions will truly help.

2. **Find out who you are in Christ.** Perhaps you are a people-pleaser like me, and you are constantly looking for others to tell you who you are. You look for praise and recognition to confirm that you are okay. This is a terrible

---

[4] You can accept Jesus right now with the help of this prayer. God isn't concerned with the exact words; He is looking for a heart change (Romans 10:9-10). It is the giving over of your life to Him that counts. Here is the prayer:

> *Jesus, I come to you right now and thank you for dying on the cross for me. Please forgive me for all of my sins. I ask you to come into my heart and be Lord of my life. Thank you for giving me eternal life. Help me to live according to your Word and be the kind of person you want me to be. In Jesus name, amen.*

It is important to start attending a Bible-believing church and read the Bible daily so you can grow. There is a lot to learn when you accept Christ as your Lord and Savior. If you prayed this prayer, I hope you will email me at *julie@momremade.com*. I would love to hear how God changed your life.

foundation, because as soon as you do something wrong, everything crumbles. Find out who God says you are and stand on that when everything else crumbles. Then you won't be shaken.

3. **Work on yourself.** At the end of the day, this is all you can control. Yourself. Reprogram how you think, act, and feel about yourself and the situation. Find the truth. God's truth, not your own version of the truth. Write Bible verses down on notecards to contradict any lies you are believing. Read them every day.

4. **Get help.** I was so angry and confused. I needed a counselor to help me unravel everything. I had to rewire my brain, which took time. If you don't want to use a counselor, try a pastor or support group, or even start by talking with a wise and trusted friend.

5. **Join a church, Sunday school and/or Bible study.** Do not forsake the fellowship of believers! Staying connected with a church and small group may be the most transformative thing you can do on a consistent basis. The community time will keep you accountable. God spoke so lovingly through my Bible studies and Sunday school class. He was soft and tender with me and sometimes convicting and corrective. In either situation, His love was lavished on me like the woman who poured oil on Jesus' feet.

6. **Pray.** Cry out to God. Ask Him to change your situation. In the Bible, when God's children cried out to Him, He answered their prayers. Pray for changed hearts. Not just theirs, but yours too. I started praying God's word. You just insert the person's name into the verse. I found this so powerful. In fact, it was life changing.

7. **Forgive.** Your part may be nothing more than to forgive. Don't discount this step. It is everything. There will never be real healing without forgiveness. This is what I had to work on the most while I was away. I wasn't just working on forgiving my parents. I was working on forgiving myself and forgiving God. I had to forgive myself for my part in the situation.

8. **Work on your relationship with your children (if you have some who are not estranged from you).** You may not be able to control your estranged relationship, but you can work to strengthen relationships with the children you do see. Be willing to humble yourself and ask what you can do to keep the communication clear and open. Listen and don't react. You don't want estrangement to continue through your family line any more.

9. **Fast.** How serious are you about mending the family break? Enough to restrict food (or something of significance) and suffer a little? You can see from my story how fasting helped move the situation along when it was

stuck. I can't promise a miracle when you fast, but I can promise God will honor the sacrifice. Wait for God to clearly show you what you should pray for during the fast. Each situation is different. If you can't restrict food, do another type of fast. You could fast from TV, social media, eating sweets, etc. Devote that time to prayer instead of your usual activity.

10. **Volunteer and/or go on mission trips.** Get your mind off yourself. I found volunteering and mission trips to be great remedies for depression, anger, and self-absorption. When you are helping others, you are not thinking about your own situation. Being others-oriented is so important. We spend too much time nursing our pain and obsessing. It just makes it worse. In fact, it is toxic.

11. **Read.** Find other people who have worked through unforgiveness or difficult family issues. See what they have done. Learn from them. Keep educating yourself. I have a list of resources I will share at the end of this book. There are podcasts, blogs, books, and sermons out there that can help too.

12. **Worship.** I found worship music and played it when I was feeling either angry or sad. It helped me to take my focus off of myself and put it on God. When I did this, it was like a balm being poured over all the raw places. Worship is a way to surrender your heart to God and

drop it in His lap. He is always so tender when we bow to Him in complete surrender and praise His name despite what we see on the surface.

13. **Find godly friends.** Surround yourself with godly people. I found a friend who had been estranged from her parents too. What a divine appointment. We got together regularly and prayed for each other and our families. It helped to have someone else to talk to outside of the family who understood. Since we started praying, both of us have reconciled with our parents. I am still in awe of how God worked in both of our situations. I also have a great group of godly girlfriends who I know love me and are there for me.

14. **Honor your parents.** While I was estranged, I had a very difficult time understanding what my responsibilities were as an estranged adult child. I felt like God was not going to give me a long life because of the commandment, "Honor your father and mother, so that you may live long in the land the Lord your God is giving you" (Exodus 20:12). I heard a sermon recently over this very subject. My pastor said "honor" literally means "heavy or weighty." To honor is to give weight to someone or grant a position of respect. It says nothing about obedience, but respect can be interpreted in a lot of ways.

How do you give weight or respect to your parents' position from afar? My pastor said that if you can't be in a relationship with your parents, it is still your responsibility to make sure you care for them in their old age. This entails two things: caring for them by forgiving them and seeing they are cared for when they cannot care for themselves. He stressed how important it is to release the rest to God.

15. Be quiet. This is really hard. All of the other steps are active. This one is passive. Being quiet means you stop wrestling with God. Put your hands down and release the situation to Him. Trust Him to work in His way and in His time. Surrender.

Closing Words

Some of you may wonder how my health is now that I have returned to my family. Currently, I am in remission and take no medicine. This is not normal for someone with Crohn's disease. (I am definitely not promoting for anyone else to stop taking medicine.) Being in remission was an unexpected surprise. And as unpredictable as Crohn's disease is, it could change at any moment. What I am saying is I have healed on many different levels. All the anger and bitterness truly affected my physical well-being. Forgiving and setting boundaries helped me to get my life back. Thankfully, I have reconciled with all family members even though all family members have not reconciled with each other.

I don't know where you are in relationship to your own family or if you are dealing with a chronic illness. If you took the time to read this book, it is likely you are experiencing some difficulties. If God can work in my life and family, He can work in yours. There is always hope when God is involved. If you don't do anything else, I encourage you to start forgiving. You will see breakthroughs from there.

My heart aches for those of you who decide not to go back to your family. Or for those of you still waiting for your adult child to come home. God hurts with you too. He knows your heart is broken. I understand there are many situations where the timing isn't right. I waited seven years before we felt ready to go back. You may be estranged from your earthly family, but you will never be ripped out from God's family. His love is unconditional. He will never fail you.

My parents and I want the body of Christ to learn from our story. Our hope is that the mistakes we made will be used for God's glory in the end. That you will find hope when your family falls apart. Our family truly believes what it says in Romans 8:28: "And we know that in all things God works for the good of those who love him, who have been called according to his purpose."

Thank you for taking the time to read my story. **I would truly appreciate a review of this book on Amazon.** Spreading the word will give more families a chance to heal and be restored.

Book Recommendations

Here is a list of books my family and I recommend. They are great resources to help you work through the different stages of healing.

- The Bible, any translation
- *The Power of Praying for Your Adult Children*, by Stormie Omartian
- *Praying God's Word*, by Beth Moore
- *Life on the Brick Pile*, by James Denison
- *How to Really Love God as Your Father*, by Deborah Newman
- *Forgive & Forget*, by Lewis B. Smedes
- *The Peacemaker and Peacemaking for Families*, by Ken Sande
- *The Return of the Prodigal Son*, by Henri Nouwen
- *Total Forgiveness*, by R. T. Kendall
- *Praying God's Will for my Daughter or Son*, by Lee Roberts
- *Through a Season of Grief*, by Bill Dunn and Kathy Leonard
- *Crucial Conversations*, by Patterson, Grenny, McMillan, and Switzler
- *Choosing Gratitude*, by Nancy Leigh DeMoss
- *When Your Child Breaks Your Heart*, by Barbara Johnson
- *Prodigals and Those Who Love Them*, by Ruth Bell Graham

Introspection

1. Will you toss this book aside or really consider your behavior with your family?
2. Will you start praying for whomever hurt you?
3. In chapter six, I talk about the real problem. If you have done any of these behaviors, will you approach those you have offended, ask forgiveness, and truly change?
4. If you are chronically ill, will you take inventory and see if you need to heal some emotional wounds?
5. If there is nothing you have really done, will you forgive?

Verses for Spiritual Warfare

James 1:22, 25

Do not merely listen to the word, and so deceive yourselves. Do what it says ... But whoever looks intently into the perfect law that gives freedom and continues in it—not forgetting what they have heard but doing it—they will be blessed in what they do.

Romans 12:2

Do not conform to the pattern of this world but be transformed by the renewing of your mind. Then you will be able to test and approve what God's will is—his good, pleasing and perfect will.

Isaiah 43:19

See, I am doing a new thing! Now it springs up; do you perceive it? I am making a way in the wilderness and streams in the wasteland.

Deuteronomy 6:18

Do what is right and good in the Lord's sight, so that it may go well with you and you may go in and take over the good land the Lord promised on oath to your ancestors.

AFTERWORD
An Interview with Julie's Mother

This is an interview with my mother, Joanne Ventura. I want to thank her for opening up her heart and sharing some words of wisdom. It is not easy to talk about such a painful part of her life. She was gracious to be so open and honest. I believe her perspective will help enlighten the adult child to the parent's point of view. I think it is important to hear both sides. It hasn't been easy walking in her shoes. For those of you with estranged children, this might also give you comfort.

Many times, the different generations do not understand one another. They both have different expectations. There has been a seismic shift in the last 40 years. Perhaps if we slow down and listen, we may understand that there are definitely two sides to any story. The older generation needs to be heard. Their feelings count.

Thanks, mom, for adding this section. I am grateful for all the hours you have spent unraveling everything that happened and working through the issues. Most of all, thank you for being willing to share your struggles publicly.

What do you think went wrong?

Pride

Pride was manifested over time. Everyone thought his point of view was the right piece of the puzzle. Julie once commented that there was a generational difference in how we handled the conflict. The younger generation says, "I don't have to put up with this!" And the older generation says, "How dare you!"

When in a conflict, it is important to humble yourself and be the first one to say, "This is what I did. (Name the offense.) I know I hurt you; I was wrong. Will you please forgive me?" Refusing to take ownership of wrong behavior halts progress. This is easy to do when there is pride. Instead, own your part and work on changing what you can. Proverbs 13:10 reminds us, "Where there is strife, there is pride, but wisdom is found in those who take advice."

Lack of Appropriate Communication

When communication ends, it is certain there can be no resolution. Continue to talk through the problems and find a suitable solution for all parties. Be flexible and understanding of other's needs. Work through your problems when they happen. When you don't, things can quickly turn into a volcanic eruption. Instead, ask what you have done. Respond in an appropriate way without letting anger rule your heart. Tell the other person you want to keep the communication open.

Bitterness

Do not allow bitterness to corrupt your life. Ephesians 4:31-32 is the guide. It says, "Get rid of all bitterness, rage and anger, brawling and slander, along with every form of malice. Be kind and compassionate to one another, forgiving each other, just as in Christ God forgave you."

If you could go back, what would you do differently?

I would consider the cost of working outside the home. Of course, the tradeoff would be the standard of living. I did not know there would be a negative cost. As a working mother, I felt it was difficult juggling family, home, work, and church. I am grateful I could work in the family business, but I felt torn to pieces at times. If I could go back, I would spend more quality time with my family. I would pursue the conversation with the offended party and ask, "What do you want and need from me?" I would dig for the answers and talk about mutual solutions.

What are some signs to look for in your relationship with an adult child that would show it is headed toward estrangement?

- Cancels previous plans.
- Doesn't make new plans.
- Conversation is guarded.
- Doesn't call.

How would you recommend others avoid this dangerous path?

If you address issues "in the flesh," you are certain to fail. What does this mean? For Christians, this means we back off, pray, and ask the Holy Spirit to guide us. Carnality wields a terrible hand. Once something like this is set in motion, I do not think you can stop it without the help of our loving Heavenly Father, who is the author of redemption and reconciliation.

What we are dealing with is a large elephant who has taken residence in the family room. As we all go up to feel the elephant, we each feel a different part of the whole. One says, "The elephant is smooth." Another person says, "It has a long trunk." The last person describes it as "very large." No one sees the entire elephant at the same time. Each draws his own conclusion from only the part he sees.

All the versions are true, but they are not the complete truth. We have to learn to be flexible and willing to see another viewpoint. Not just our own. John 8:31-32 emphasizes, "If you hold to my teaching, you are really my disciples. Then you will know the truth, and the truth will set you free."

What advice would you give specifically to parents to help them prevent this kind of family rift?

Ken Sande, in his book *The Peacemaker*, says there are four primary causes of conflict:[5]

- Misunderstanding resulting from poor communications
- Difference in values, goals, gifts, calling, priorities, expectations, interests or opinions
- Competition over limited resources, such as time and money
- Sinful attitudes and habits that lead to sinful words and actions

5   Sande, Ken. *The Peace Maker*. Baker Books, 2004, p. 30.

Communication is something we all have to work on ALL the time. I would tell parents to regularly communicate with their adult children. Spend even more time listening. It is important to make sure all sides are heard.

Make it safe for your adult child to disagree. Be willing to "agree to disagree" peaceably. Move on without allowing it to harm the relationship. I would also recommend modeling forgiveness for your children. They do what you do. If you are unforgiving, chances are they will be unforgiving too.

How did you forgive?

It is best to forgive offenses immediately. If we do not choose instant forgiveness, then it becomes a process that is difficult to untangle. Forgiveness frees us. Only a free person can live with an uneven score. Free people can choose to start over with someone who has hurt them. Free people can heal the memory of hurt or hatred.

The first step is to want to forgive. Please do not be deceived—forgiveness is a choice we make daily. Nobody can make us forgive. Sometimes I had to pray, "Lord, help me want to forgive." I did not give up, because I knew who the real enemy was. It is not a person. Ephesian 6:12 tells us, "For our struggle is not against flesh and blood, but against the rulers, against the authorities, against the powers of this dark world and against the spiritual forces of evil in the heavenly realms."

Once the choice is determined, I have found the only way to forgive the hard things is to ask Jesus to help us forgive as He has forgiven us. He will meet us at our point of need. Matthew 6:12, 14-15 is the example: "And forgive us our debts, as we also have forgiven our debtors. ... For if you forgive other people when they sin against you, your heavenly Father will also forgive you. But if you do not forgive others their sins, your Father will not forgive your sins."

Jesus died so that we may have His forgiveness. Without it, we have no relationship with Him. Remember, feeling follows action. Eventually, I did feel I had forgiven everyone but myself. I was the hardest one to forgive. God encouraged me through the darkest days, assuring me I was valuable and that He would be with me through the trial. He kept His word.

When forgiving, there are five questions to consider:

- Is there emotional churning or obsessing?
- Is it hard to ask God to bless those who have wronged you?
- Do you want others to know (friends and family) how you were hurt? This is a big one, because we want to expose the person we believe wronged us.
- Is it hard to focus on the person's good qualities?
- Do you want to seek revenge, to punish, or to get even?

Instead of allowing your flesh to rule, I suggest you intentionally work on doing these things:

- Rest and relinquish the situation to God.
- Ask God to bless those who have wronged you.
- Focus on your own sin and God's forgiveness.
- Show gratefulness to God for each person in the situation.
- Desire to see restoration.

"'In your anger, do not sin': Do not let the sun go down while you are still angry, and do not give the devil a foothold" (Ephesians 4:26-27).

What did you do all the years your adult children were gone?

I cannot say life went on "as usual," because it did not. We had to adjust and make a new life without the missing family members. We continued to pray and be involved in church and the community. My husband and I opened a bed and breakfast. It helped us to stay busy. We decided to be grateful for what we did have instead of focusing on what we did not have.

How did the estrangement affect the family?

I wish I could tell you the effect on the family was contained, but it had a ripple effect. Every decision a family member makes, past or present, affects everyone else. Two families emerged—"Them" and "Us." The conflict put some of the family members in the middle many times. They had to choose who to be with or who to invite to a family function. We missed our oldest grandson's wedding. That was hard on all of us. Everyone felt the unfortunate effects of estrangement.

As parents, we model to our children life's lessons. When there is unresolved conflict, the lesson learned is "fight or flight." Thus, it passes from one generation to another. The next generation just repeats what they learned from their parents. Stop the generational curses and do things differently.

How did you get through the holidays and special occasions?

The holidays were hard! However, we continued with our lives. We still celebrated the holidays and invited anyone who was interested in coming. We sent gifts until we were asked to stop. We tried to stay within the boundaries of the estrangement. We did not want to add more fuel to the fire.

Hidden hurts close hearts. We had to go through the holidays and not around them. We had to grieve the losses. We learned to accept with joy what God had for us at the time—the family who did come to celebrate with us. The past was over, and we could not redo it, only replay it.

A counselor once said to me, "If you have one foot in the present and one foot in the past, you seriously mess up the present." We worked on staying in the present and being grateful for what God gave us each day.

What do you recommend other moms do when their adult children leave?

- Pray and continue to pray.
- Humble yourself.
- If possible, keep healthy communication lines open.
- Be vulnerable and available.
- Repent of your sin. If you do not know what it is, ask God to show you.
- Stop all blaming.
- Apologize for your part in the estrangement, as it becomes clear.
- Set boundaries.

How did you deal with the anger, shame, and embarrassment?

Really, we wanted to run away and hide. Some people thought the very worst about us. We recognized that we had hurting children. Much of it was our fault. We asked God to forgive us and change us. We came to understand we gave our kids everything we had to give—physically, spiritually, and emotionally. We did the best we could; if we could have done better, we would have. We could not give them what we did not have.

We daily offered the situation up to God. We refused to let other opinions guide our lives. We quit trying to do anything but pray. God's way is found in Hebrews 12:14-15: "Make every effort to live in peace with everyone and to be holy; without holiness no one will see the Lord. See to it that no one falls short of the grace of God and that no bitter root grows up to cause trouble and defile many."

Do you have any final words of advice?

I will not tell you the past years have been easy ones, but God has always seen us through. I know it is in the valleys where we grow, not on the mountaintops. My prayer for each of you reading this book is that the Holy Spirit will touch you and heal you physically, emotionally, and spiritually. Jesus knows your pain. You can rest in Him.

ABOUT Julie Plagens

Julie Plagens is a wife, mother, teacher, blogger, and author. Before she married, she taught speech, drama, and English in the Richardson Independent School District. After she married, she became a stay-at-home mom. Julie has spent time volunteering for many years doing Vacation Bible School programs, food distribution, and door-to-door witnessing. Now that her two children are grown, she is a substitute teacher for a private school and works intermittently for her husband's business. Julie and her husband have been married for 25 years and live in Dallas, Texas.

After a heartbreaking estrangement from her family, Julie realized she was not alone in her feelings of shame and her struggles to interact with family in healthy ways. Now that she has reconciled with her parents, she wishes to help others find hope when they experience a family rift. When Julie is not talking about reconciliation, she is sharing helpful tips on her blog about family, parenting, marriage, education, and faith.

Mom Remade

ENCOURAGING MOTHERS...FROM THE OTHER SIDE OF PARENTHOOD

MomRemade.com

Made in the USA
Monee, IL
27 February 2025

13098056R00094